Tools of the Imagination

Tools of the Imagination: Drawing Tools and Technologies from the Eighteenth Century to the Present

Susan C. Piedmont-Palladino, editor

PRINCETON ARCHITECTURAL PRESS, NEW YORK

Published by
Princeton Architectural Press
37 East Seventh Street
New York, New York 10003

For a free catalog of books, call 1.800.722.6657.
Visit our web site at www.papress.com.

The publication of *Tools of the Imagination: Drawing Tools and Technologies from the Eighteenth Century
to the Present* is made possible by Autodesk

Page vi: Specimens of Drawing Paper (in Allegorical wood-cut). Reprinted from *Ackerman's Repository,
Supplement to Vol. III* (1810).

For the National Building Museum
Publication manager: Reed Haslach
Graphics coordination: Matthew Kuhnert

For Princeton Architectural Press
Editing: Linda Lee
Design: mgmt. design, Brooklyn, New York

Special thanks to: Nettie Aljian, Sara Bader, Dorothy Ball, Nicola Bednarek, Janet Behning, Becca Casbon,
Penny (Yuen Pik) Chu, Russell Fernandez, Pete Fitzpatrick, Jan Haux, Clare Jacobson, John King,
Mark Lamster, Nancy Eklund Later, Katharine Myers, Lauren Nelson Packard, Scott Tennent, Jennifer
Thompson, Paul Wagner, Joseph Weston, and Deb Wood of Princeton Architectural Press —Kevin C.
Lippert, publisher

Library of Congress Cataloging-in-Publication Data
Tools of the imagination : drawing tools and technologies from the eighteenth century to the present /
Susan Piedmont-Palladino, editor.
    p. cm.
 Includes bibliographical references.
 ISBN-13: 978-1-56898-599-2 (hardcover : alk. paper)
 1. Architectural drawing—Technique. 2. Drawing instruments. I. Piedmont-Palladino, Susan.
 NA2708.T66 2006
 720'.284—dc22
                                                        2006012497

To Joseph Donlan Piedmont, 1928–2005

SUPPLEMENT TO
Vol. III.—June 1810.
HONI SOIT MAL Y PENSE
DIEU ET MON DROIT
1
2
3
4

The Repository

Of Arts, Literature, Commerce, Manufactures, Fashions, and Politics,

SPECIMENS OF DRAWING PAPERS.

R. Ackermann, 101, *Strand, London.*

Contents

Foreword

Tools are among the most reliable gauges of human progress. The broad stages of early human history, in fact, are identified primarily by the types of tools developed and used during each cultural period, such as the Stone Age and the Bronze Age. The tools of a given age are revealing indicators not only of a society's achievements but also of its aspirations and limitations.

The National Building Museum's exhibition TOOLS OF THE IMAGINATION was conceived as an exploration of the architectural design process and the varied implements employed in that practice. The result was an engaging survey of items—from simple pencils, to elaborate devices for constructing perspectives, to astonishingly powerful software—whose qualities and significance were illuminated through the presentation of drawings, digital renderings, and models that they made possible. Visitors to the exhibition emerged with a clearer understanding of how architects and other designers cultivate, test, and express complex ideas.

This book uses the exhibition as a springboard for deeper exploration of several issues. In his essay, Paul Emmons brings a fresh perspective to the humble pencil, celebrating its unparalleled utility as a communication tool. David V. Thompson offers the unique viewpoint of the avid collector of drawing tools, reminding us that such devices often have remarkable personal significance to an architect. Phillip Bernstein's essay focuses on revolutionary new tools and strategies in the design industry, such as Building Information Modeling (BIM), in which the mere representation of a building as lines on paper is superseded by a fully integrated database, of which the "drawing" is just a legible expression. William J. Mitchell offers some final thoughts on the nature of drawing in both the analog and the digital realms.

In addition to these essayists, the National Building Museum thanks all of the people who contributed to the exhibition and this book. The exhibition content was masterfully developed by Susan Piedmont-Palladino, an architect and professor at Virginia Tech's Washington-Alexandria Architecture Consortium, who served as guest curator on this and other projects for the Museum. She worked closely with curatorial associate Reed Haslach. Piedmont-Palladino and Haslach brought the subject matter to life in the Museum's galleries and managed its transformation into book form. The exhibition was designed by Andrew Pettiti of Knowtis Design and was constructed by the Museum's exhibition team, led by Hank Griffith. The book was designed by Stephanie Church of mgmt. design and published in cooperation with Princeton Architectural Press.

The Museum enjoyed excellent guidance on this project from an Advisory Committee led by co-chairs Carol Bartz, executive chairman of the board of Autodesk, Inc., and Greg Bentley, chief executive officer of Bentley Systems, Inc.

Projects such as these are not possible without significant outside financial support, and the Museum is grateful to all its contributors. In particular, the Museum thanks Autodesk, Inc., for its generous support of this publication.

On behalf of the National Building Museum, I thank all of the dedicated and, yes, imaginative team members who made TOOLS OF THE IMAGINATION possible.

Chase W. Rynd, Executive Director
National Building Museum

Installation view of the TOOLS
OF THE IMAGINATION exhibition at
the National Building Museum,
Washington, D.C., March 5
through October 10, 2005

Preface

We all use tools every day of our lives—coffeemaker at breakfast, cell phones throughout the day, perhaps a computer or a pipe wrench at work, and then a corkscrew for the evening wine with supper or a spoon for our bowl of soup. Tools are the means by which we attain the results of our imaginings. A thought or dream occurs to us, and we reach for our tools to transform that wish into reality.

TOOLS OF THE IMAGINATION began as an attempt to gain access to the relationship between the physical world we shape and build and the desires that motivate us. How do architects record their visions, develop them, and ultimately instruct others in their construction? How have architect's tools shaped the buildings we inhabit, and how have architects' visions shaped their tools? In the pages that follow, you will see architects' tools across time and understand the tasks that they were intended to accomplish.

In the past, each building was a custom-made object because the tools to reproduce objects—or drawings— were very limited. The architects, or master stonemasons, who envisioned a sheltering structure, did not often make elaborate drawings with sophisticated tools. Instead, they relied on canons of proportion, systems of order, and ornament that could be written or orally passed between generations.

The industrial age brought with it machines capable of reproducing objects and greater availability of tools to achieve more advanced operations. First the pencil, then the ubiquitous tracing paper and duplicating tools began to emerge, so that information could be reproduced and more widely transmitted. Other tools, aimed at drawing certain kinds of lines or types of ornament, joined the toolbox as well. By the beginning of the twentieth century,

American cities and towns were exploding in scale and population. The demand to design and build to accommodate this rapid growth was strong, and the architect's toolbox and tool technology increasingly serviced the frenzy of construction.

Historically, architects used one version or another of a reiterative process: sketch, overlay transparent paper, resketch, and revise. Repeat this over and over until the drawing and the vision touch one another. Instructing others on how to build the dream involved the use of transparent paper or, later, sheets of nearly clear Mylar plastic to ensure that the object was precise and consistent in plan, elevation, and section. By the last quarter of the twentieth century, architects had, in addition to the familiar blue-printing machines, large-scale copiers capable of rapidly making copies of full-sized drawing sheets. But the real change came with the advent of the computer.

It is the computer and computer-aided design (CAD) that have radically transformed the practice of architecture. Now, we seem to have come full circle: from a time when all buildings were custom made, to the standardization and mass production of the industrial age, and now, with digital technologies, back to the customization of each building or object. The computer, coupled with the Internet, allows the instantaneous transfer of particularized information among project teammates, clients, builders, and building managers. In so many ways, architects can work almost anywhere, hooked together in the ether of cyberspace.

Now the boisterous forms of bold, curving, crumpled architecture can easily be managed with computers. What were once only two-dimensional tools to describe three-

dimensional architecture have now become electronic
tools that allow architects to work throughout the entire
process fully in three dimensions. It seems as though the
limits of what we can imagine, and construct, have been
radically expanded because of our tools.

New tools have brought new questions. Historians ask, if
we no longer have drawings on paper, how do we preserve
the architect's work? How can any of us see the development of ideas across time when the reiterative process has
been superseded? Can the hand of the designer still be
detected in the drawings? We mount the beautiful pencil
drawings of Frank Lloyd Wright or Mies Van der Rohe on
the walls of our museums, admiring them as the beautiful
objects they are. Now what?

Other questions also come to mind. How do we understand the difference between what our tools allow us to do
and what we *should* do to make and remake our buildings,
and our cities and towns? Do our new tools allow us
to build more sustainably, more humanely, creating better
places to live and work? TOOLS OF THE IMAGINATION
succeeds in provoking these questions and invites us to
search for answers. Tools of any trade are windows into
that world and take us behind the scene. We can examine
how tools make the seemingly effortless possible. TOOLS
OF THE IMAGINATION shows us how architects turn dreams
of once-unimagined worlds into the places where we lead
our daily lives.

Howard S. Decker, FAIA

Introduction

"I've always wanted to be an architect, but I just couldn't draw a straight line." Many would-be architects have been discouraged from the design professions because of their perceived inability to draw a straight line, a circle, a convincing perspective, or realistic shadows. The architect's ability to put compelling images of future buildings and cities on paper, or on screen, is remarkable, but it is not magic.

It is fascinating to watch the construction of a building, but one rarely sees its design. On the construction site, every component has its craftworker, and every worker has a set of appropriate tools—from hammers to cranes—to turn piles of parts of materials into a work of architecture. Like the builder, the architect needs the right tools for the job. Before the tools of construction ever arrive on the scene, the architect deploys a different set of tools to design, develop, and document the building-to-be. These are the tools of the imagination. The architect's work takes place out of public view on the pages of sketchbooks, drawing tables, and computer screens of the studio. The newest tool, the computer, is really an entirely new toolbox full of software to solve old and new problems.

These challenges have been solved manually, mechanically, sometimes chemically, and, now, electronically. Problems of geometry are fundamental to drawing, and some of the most familiar tools are directed toward their solution: compasses, straightedge rulers, measuring devices, to name a few. But making a convincing drawing, one that allows the viewer see what is possible, demands another set of tools that assist in the representation of perspective space, light, and shadows. Finally, the architect needs tools to produce, reproduce, alter, and document the information as it becomes a set of instructions for building.

Every tool was at one time the new thing, the high-tech solution to a persistent problem. Before long, what once was high tech becomes standard, and we begin to look for the next new thing. While our current new thing, the computer and its suites of software, has radically changed how architects work, to view the present as completely severed from the past obscures the thread of continuity in our relationship with technology. That relationship is played out repeatedly as the new becomes old, the indispensable useless, the special ordinary, and the ordinary special, as need and desire coax tools from our imaginations that in turn serve our imaginations. No doubt our workstations and laptops, loaded with the newest visualization software, will someday appear as quaint to our descendants as pantographs, perspectagraphs, and blueprints do now.

This volume, a companion and sequel to the exhibition of the same name held at the National Building Museum between March and October 2005, reveals how architects, engineers, and designers create the images that they do. Some of these artifacts, like the ellipsograph, are now more beautiful than useful; some, like computer stations, are too useful to be seen aesthetically. Others, like Thomas Jefferson's gridded paper and Paul Rudolph's colored pencils, are so remarkably unremarkable that we wonder how they escaped the trash heap. Still others, from our recent past, straddle the strange boundary between nostalgia and nuisance. Architects of a certain age will recognize this quality in the tools from the office of Tod Williams Billie Tsien Architects (TWBTA), just swept off the drawing boards to make room for the new screen. It is through the mastery of the full range of tools that the images in the architect's mind are translated into drawings and models, and from the drawings and the models into buildings. Whether a simple pencil or computer software, these tools give form to the wishes and the instructions of the architect, but they are also active shapers of what is possible.

Susan Piedmont-Palladino

Not all of us can draw two figures, mirror images, using both hands, as architect Louis Kahn does. Yet the desire for symmetry—whether at the scale of ornament or building mass—has been a constant in architecture. The evolution of tools to make a reverse image of a drawing is indicative of the evolutions of all drawing technologies. "The antigraph is the only instrument for drawing parts of a figure the reverse hand to the original," claimed prolific toolmaker William Ford Stanley in 1888. Stanley's invention, the antigraph, did mechanically what Kahn could do by hand. The principle of the antigraph is simple enough, but its use actually requires a bit more ambidexterity than most of us have. Far easier is the keystroke that instructs the computer to copy_mirror.

left
Reproduction of a nineteenth-century antigraph

opposite
Louis I. Kahn
ca. 1965. Photograph by Martin Rich.

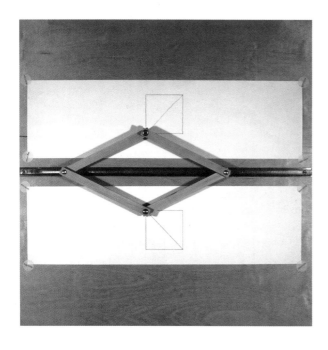

Timeline

1400

1400s
Paper becomes common in Europe.

1500

1560
Graphite is first mined in England.

1600

1600
Origin of orthogonal drawings

1600
Elliptical trammel, simplest of the ellipse tools, is invented.

1603
Pantograph is invented.

1662
Friedrich Staedtler, a carpenter in Nuremberg, gives birth to the modern pencil.

1669
Sir Christopher Wren invents a perspectograph.

1700

1700
Screw-adjustable ruling pens are invented.

1700
Scissor-jointed parallel rule is invented.

1720s
T-square and drawing board become standard drafting tools.

mid-1700s
London becomes center of mathematical- and drawing-instrument making.

1760
Volute compass is invented.

1761
Founding of Faber-Castell, makers of pencils

1765
Inventor James Watt designs a portable and foldable perspectograph.

1767
First use of gum or rubber eraser, discovered by Joseph Priestly

1771
Rolling parallel rule is invented.

1790–1810
Ellipsograph is invented.

1791
Helicograph illustrated in George Adams's *Geometrical and Graphical Essays*

1795
French chemist and inventor N. J. Conte (France) develops the process for hardening graphite by adding clay.

1800

1814
British architect and mathematician Peter Nicholson invents the centrolinead.

1816
Metric measuring is adopted by Holland.

1819
John Farey invents Mr. Peacock's Delineator, a perspective aid.

1825
Laid paper first manufactured by machine

1830
Edinburg Encyclopedia describes the familiar grades of graphite.

1840
Tracing paper becomes common.

1840
Specialized ruling pens invented for cartographers and railway engineers

1840s
Wood pulp introduced into paper production

1848
Immigration of skilled instrument makers to United States from Germany and England.

1853
W. F. Stanley manufactures wood "set squares," now known as triangles.

1857
H. Johnson patents the volutor.

1860
Slopes and batters, specialized triangles for railway embankments, are invented.

1860
W. F. Stanley markets the French curve, based on sixteenth-century ship makers' curved templates.

1866
Weighted flexible curves, weights, and splines appear in W. F. Stanley's catalog.

1866
Conchoidograph, which draws flutes on a classical column in entasis, is invented.

1866
W. F. Stanley publishes *Mathematical Drawing & Measuring Instruments*.

1867
William Keuffel & Hermann Esser (K&E) sets up shop in New York.

1867
Faber-Castell improves pencils with encased and refillable holders.

late 1800s
Parabolagraph, a rare instrument for drawing parabolas, is invented.

1880
Blueprinting becomes commercially available.

1900

1900
Last sighting of a sector, which gave way to the slide rule.

1900
Retailers start to sell tools, office supplies, reprographic services.

1920
Adjustable triangle first appears in clear celluloid.

1924
W. F. Stanley's catalog shows a parallel motion rule strung on piano wire.

1932
Graphos develops the first technical pen with twelve interchangeable ruling blades.

1932
Inventor Arthur Dremel of Racine, Wisconsin, invents the electric eraser.

1940
Drop-action clutch pencil is invented.

1952
Wilhelm Riepe of Hamburg, Germany, founder of Rotring Pens, introduces Rapidograph pens with cylindrical nibs.

1952
Dupont develops Mylar polyester drawing film.

1953
Technical compasses and accessories are mass marketed and produced.

1960
British manufacturing of drawing instruments comes to an end.

1960
Quick-set compass with wing arc or horizontal screw to set and hold is invented.

1960
Compass with attachments for technical pens instead of ruling pens is invented.

1963
Ivan Sutherland develops Sketchpad.

1960s
The beginnings of commercially available computer-aided design (CAD) systems.

1970s
Staedtler and Faber-Castell produce inexpensive mass-market tools.

1972
Metric line thicknesses are introduced by Rotring.

1977
Special moisture-holding cap for technical pens is invented.

1980
Nonclogging inks, tungsten, and ceramic tips for technical pens are invented.

1980s
Pen plotter is invented.

1980
Haff manufactures the last-known acrylic ellipsograph.

1982
First release of AutoCAD, called AutoCAD 80, by Autodesk.

1983
Introduction of the laser plotter.

1986
First release of MicroStation by Bentley Systems.

1987
First release of AutoCAD10 with three-dimensional capability.

1988
3D Systems introduces commercial stereolithography, otherwise known as "3D printing."

1991
Chris Yessios and Dave Kropp develop Form Z.

1997
Irwin Jungreis and Leonid Raiz develop Revit.

1999
W. F. Stanley goes out of business.

2000

2000
Brad Schell develops SketchUp.

Circles and Spheres

Contemporary architects have access to an extraordinary array of tools, but their studios and workspaces are likely to contain tools that would have been familiar to Thomas Jefferson: triangles and compasses share desk space with laptops and scanners. Because the rules of geometry are unchanged, compasses remain useful, though architects rarely exploit their full potential. The name of this familiar two-legged drawing instrument originates from the Latin word *compassare* (to pace off or to measure). Walking across a drawing, the legs of the compass can pace a line, locate a point, bisect an angle, and, of course, construct a circle.

Compasses remain useful for drawing circles, but complex curvilinear geometries require more complex tools. Helicographs, ellipsographs, and volutors are just some of the unique tools invented in the past to draw specific curvilinear forms, such as cones, ellipses, and spirals. Each of these drawing tasks arises or vanishes with changing tastes and construction technologies.

The volutor, invented in 1857 by H. Johnson, illustrates one of the constants of technological innovation, what historian of technology Carl Mitcham calls "efforts to save effort." The classical revival of the eighteenth and nineteenth centuries had brought the Ionic column capital back to the drawing board. Previously, constructing a spiral, the underlying geometry of the Ionic volute, had been accomplished using a compass in a series of steps involving locating center points and striking arcs in a specific sequence. It was accurate, but hardly quick enough to serve the rising demand for buildings in the nineteenth century. The effort to save effort was the invention of the volutor, an elegant device that allowed a smooth construction of a spiral, rather than the sequence of discrete steps, described exhaustively in William Salmon's treatise *Palladio Londonensis* (1745). To the modern reader, this litany of steps is almost as impenetrable as computer code, and it is fundamentally the same thing: each is a set of instructions that, when executed correctly, will result in a predictable outcome. One can imagine the glee with which the younger generation of classicists embraced the volutor as the older generation mourned the loss of the knowledge of spiral construction. The volutor was fated to a short life. No sooner had it been developed that the entire culture of architecture, and the manufacture of tools, changed forever. Classical architecture receded from fashion and the clean lines and pure geometries of the modern movement returned drawing to the fundamental tools.

Now, all of these problems and others are solved deep inside the computer. The multitasking compass still paces, measures, and constructs circles, whereas the computer has teased these functions apart into different tasks. The "draw circle" command no longer belongs to the same tool set as measuring. The digital tool is a tool once removed from the drawing problems. The code itself is the tool.

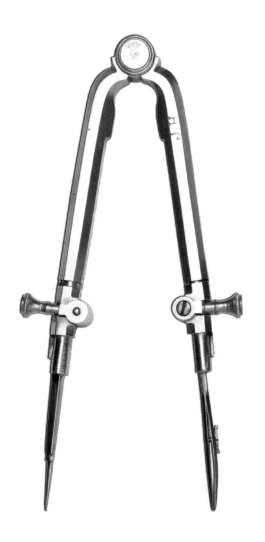

left and below
Pillar folding compass
(England), ca. 1850. Nickel-silver, steel; 4¼ x 1⅝ x ¾ in.

opposite
**Monticello: ionic portico
and dome, recto**
Thomas Jefferson, ca. 1778.
Ink on paper, 7¹⁵/₁₆ x 6¹⁵/₁₆ in.

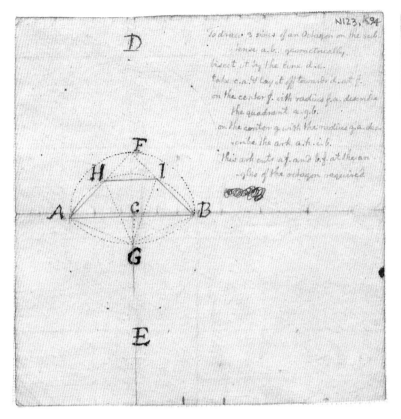

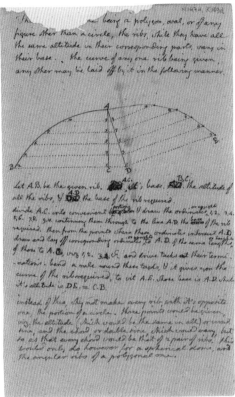

opposite, top
Tubular compass in case
(England), ca. 1890. Nickel-
silver, steel, with Morrocan
leather case; 15¾ x 3½ x 1⅛ in.

opposite, bottom
Beam compass
(France), ca. 1790. Silver, steel,
ebony; 9¾ x 2 x ½ in.

left
**Monticello: drawing
octagons**
Thomas Jefferson, 1771.
Ink on paper, 4⁵⁄₁₆ x 4³⁄₈ in.

right
Monticello: curve of dome
Thomas Jefferson, ca. 1796.
Ink on paper, 7¹⁵⁄₁₆ x 4½ in.

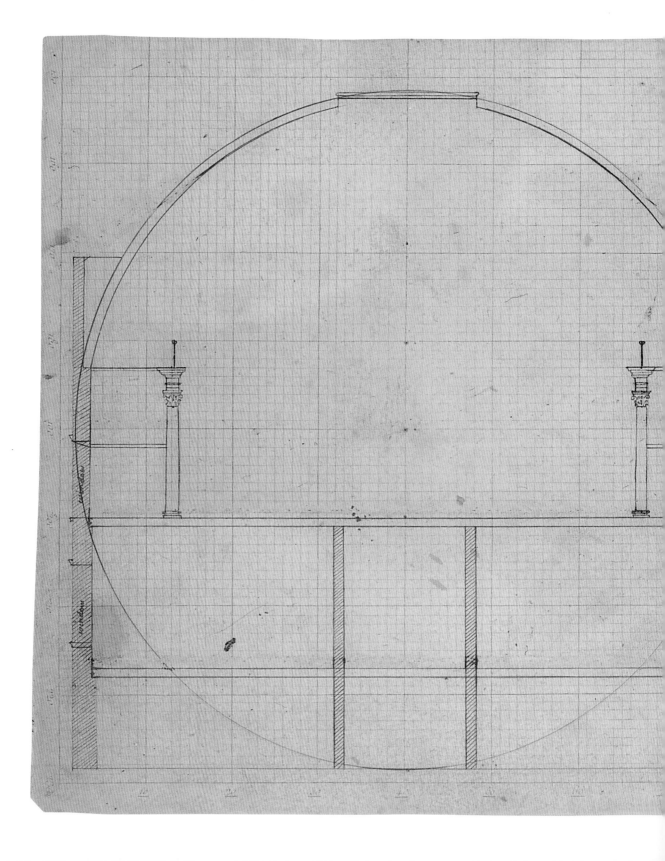

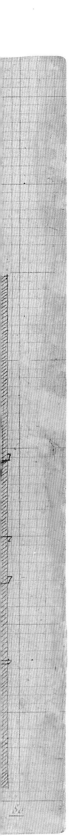

opposite

Section of the Rotunda
Thomas Jefferson, 1819.
Pricking, iron-gall ink on
laid paper engraved with
coordinate lines; 8¾ x 8¾ in.

below

Compasses
Reprinted from George
Adams, *Geometrical and
Graphical Essays*, 3rd ed.
(London: W. Glendinning,
1803), plate 1.

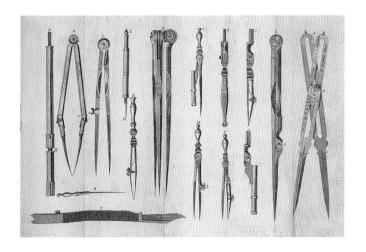

Pocket cased set
Peter & George Dollond, 1810.
Silver, ivory, steel; 7 x 3½ in.
(assembled).

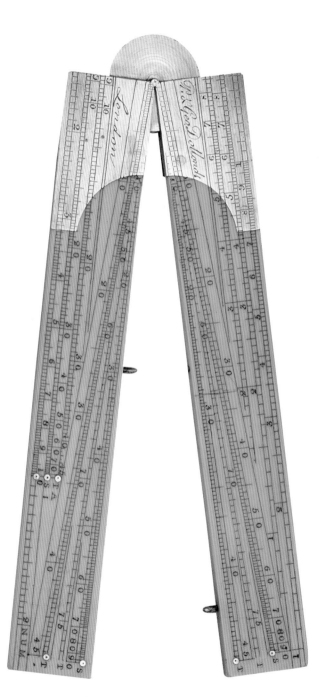

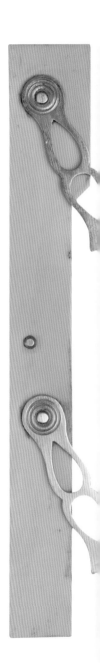

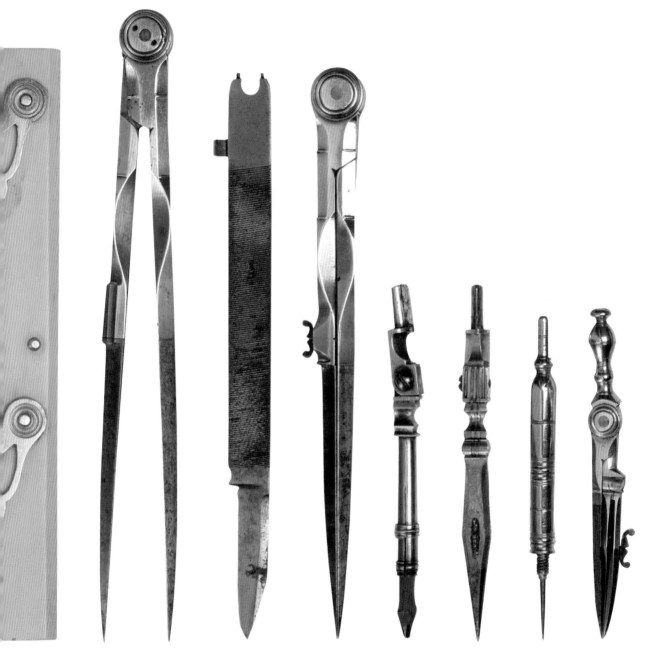

Instruction for constructing an Ionik Volute with a compass, from William Salmon's *Palladio Londinensis* of 1745:

"First draw the Astragal AB, and though the Middle thereof the line EF; then from the Top of the Abacus, let fall, perpendicular to the former, another line passing through the Center of the Circle, or Eye, of the Volute, as GH. Within this Circle are twelve Centers marked 1, 2, 3, 4, & c. to 12, on which the Contour of the Volute is described, and are thus to be found. Describe a Geometrical Square whose Diagonals are one in the Horizontal Line, and the other in the Perpendicular Line, crossing each other in the Center of the Eye; from the Middle of the Sides of this Square draw two lines which divide the Square into four, and each Line being divided into six Parts, gives the twelve Centers, or Points, required as they are numbered in the eye of the Volute. To describe the Volute, open your compasses from No. 1 (in the Eye of the Volute) to the intersection of the Perpendicular and the lower part of the Abacus, and draw a Quarter of a Circle, viz. Continue it till it meets the Horizontal Line EF.

Secondly, On the Point 2, place your Compasses, and open them to the Arch last described, and continue the Arch-Line till it meets the Perpendicular GH.

Thirdly, On the Point 3, place your Compasses and open them to the Arch last described, and continue the Arch-Line till it meet the Perpendicular EF...

In like manner you may turn it about till you have gone through all twelve Centers, which will describe the contour of the Volute as required. The inside Line, or Border, is described by a second Draught, in the same Manner as the former, only placing the fixed Foot of the Compasses in the twelve other Centers, very near the first, viz. at one fifth part of the Distance that is between the former, reckoning towards the Center of the Eye; and these twelve Centers are represented by the twelve Points in the Eye of the Volute made larger that any other, on which the inside Line may be described as required."

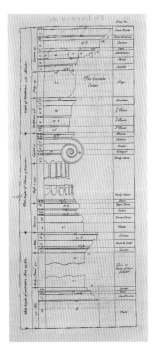

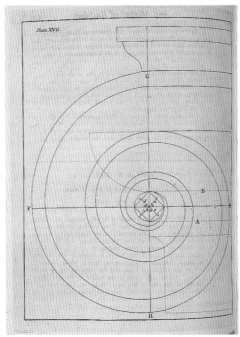

opposite, left
The Ionick Order
Reprinted from William Salmon,
Palladio Londinensis (London:
S. Birt, 1748), plate VI.

opposite, right
Diagram of a Spiral
Reprinted from William Salmon,
Palladio Londinensis (London:
S. Birt, 1748), plate XVII.

below
Volutor
ca. 1858. Brass, horn,
porcelain, thread, steel;
8.5 x 30 x 19.5 cm (overall).

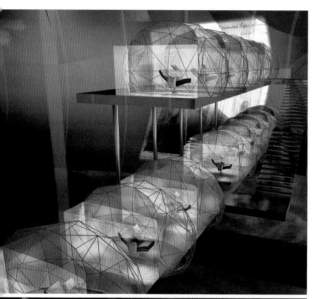

The Association for Computer Aided Design in Architecture (ACADIA) launched its first design competition in 1998, challenging architects to rethink a traditional building type—the library—with nontraditional tools. For their winning solution, Ryan Chin, Jeffrey Tsui, and Constance Lai, architecture students at the Massachusetts Institute of Technology, proposed a Library for One. Working first in sketches and clay models, the team moved quickly into the digital design environment, where they could wield the tools best suited to represent a library for the information age. Chin envisions a future where the architect would no longer hunch over a drawing board or a screen but would be able to manipulate virtual objects. Up to the elbows in virtual space, the architect could design like an orchestra conductor, summoning materials and spaces to perform.

opposite
Group Research Spaces
Ryan Chin and Jeffrey Tsui,
from *Library for the
Information Age*, 1998

left, top
**Pod: The Digitally Mediated
Reading Room for One**
Ryan Chin and Jeffrey Tsui,
from *Library for the
Information Age*, 1998

left, bottom
Pod Interior
Ryan Chin and Jeffrey Tsui,
from *Library for the
Information Age*, 1998

The Line

In architectural drawing, a line is never just a line. Whether it is freehand or drafted, physical or electronic, dashed, dotted, or snapped, a line always represents something else. It is a wall, the edge of a step, a change of ceiling height, an invisible guide to locating columns. The construction of a single straight line demands the simplest tool set: a surface, an edge, and an instrument to make the mark. Drafters practiced the technique of twirling the pencil along the straightedge to yield the perfect line. Being able to draw a straight line, whether patiently and delicately by hand or along a straightedge, is only half of the problem. Making it a good line, with the right "weight," a precise beginning and end, consistent and clear, takes practice and specific tools. The standardization of line weights—the differential thickness of lines that indicate their meaning—was a quest of instrument makers. Before technical pens, before the computer, line weight came literally from the weight of the hand of the draftsman: more weight, fatter line; less weight, lighter line. While this gave infinite possibilities, it also meant that control was a difficult skill to master.

Graphite, ink, and plastic lead have yielded to pixels while linen, trace, and Mylar have yielded to the screen, where drawing a line is not really drawing "on" anything at all. The mouse and keystrokes are indifferent to the weight of the hand, and computer-generated lines divorce the act of making the line from its appearance on paper. The task of getting the glowing lines off the screen and onto a sheet of paper spurred a series of inventions in output devices; the final "plot," the physical output, executes the instructions for drawing the line.

Lines belong to drawing, however, not to architecture itself. The rise of Building Information Modeling software recasts the computer as a tool of data representation rather than drafting and will challenge the very definition of a "set of drawings." Increasingly, output is not limited to paper: so-called "3D" printers and CAD-CAM technologies translate digital instructions directly into models, prototypes, and, ultimately, actual building elements.

Set squares, more commonly called triangles, serve two purposes: constructing angled lines and straight lines perfectly perpendicular to the T-square line. Currently manufactured in standardized fixed angles of 30/60 and 45/45 and an adjustable version, set squares first appeared in the seventeenth century and became common in the nineteenth. The T-square first emerged in an illustration in William Salmon's *Palladio Londinensis* (1734 edition), where he describes how to make one:

"First, a Drawing-Board A, which should be made of wainscot, Mahogany, or some other hard wood, about 19 Inches in Length, and 16 Inches in Width, or any Size that the largeness of Paper you use may require, with Pieces glewed [sic] on to each end to keep it from warping. A tee-square B should be made, with its Stem 8, 10, or 12 Inches long and an Inch and half wide, in the middle of which you must fix a Tongue or Blade, as thin as you well can, the thinner the better, taking care that it be fixed in at right Angles with the Stem, and as long as your Drawing Board."

opposite and above
30/60 set squares
ca. 1900, manufactured by
Dietzgen, Chicago, Illinois.
Mahogany, ebony; 8 in. length.

right
Adjustable T-Square
ca. 1900. Mahogany, steel;
10 x 27 in. (overall).

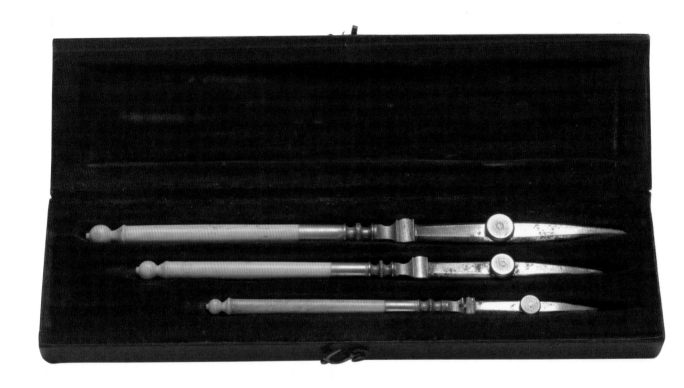

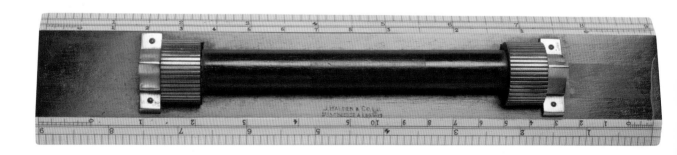

opposite, top
Ruling pen set
ca. 1900, manufactured by
Kern, Arrau, Switzerland.
Nickel-silver, ivory, steel;
6¾ x 1¾ x 1 in.

opposite, bottom
Rolling parallel rule
ca. 1900, manufactured by
John Haldon & Co., Ltd.,
Manchester, England. Ebony,
ivory, brass; 9¼ x 2 x 1 in.

right, top
**Mies van der Rohe in
Crown Hall**
ca. 1955. Gelatin-silver print.
Photograph by Hedrich
Blessing [HB-18506-14].

right, center and following page
**South, north, and east
elevations, Illinois Institute
of Technology, Crown Hall,
Chicago, Illinois**
Ludwig Mies van der Rohe,
1954. Blueprint, 36 x 48 in.

right, bottom
**Main-floor plan,
Illinois Institute of
Technology Crown Hall**
Ludwig Mies van der Rohe,
1954. Blueprint, 36 x 48 in.

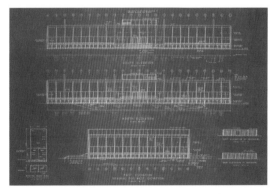

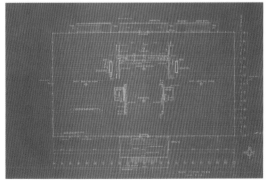

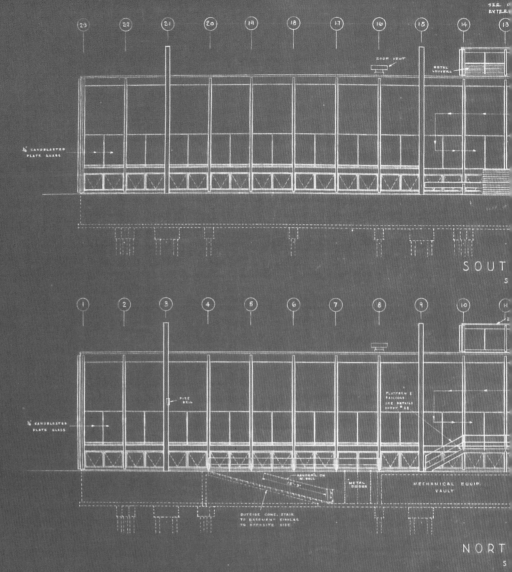

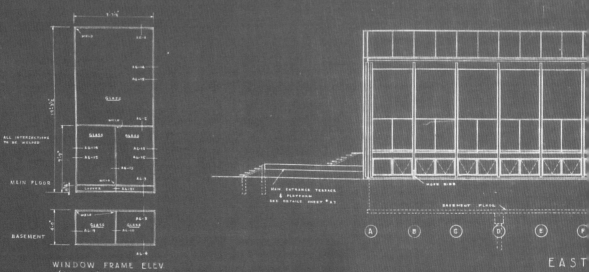

SOUT

NORT

EAST
REVERSE FO

WINDOW FRAME ELEV.
(SHOWING 1" THICK BAR STOCK ONLY)
SCALE 3/8" = 1'-0"

MAIN FLOOR

BASEMENT

ALL INTERSECTIONS
TO BE WELDED

GLASS

GLASS   GLASS

GLASS   GLASS

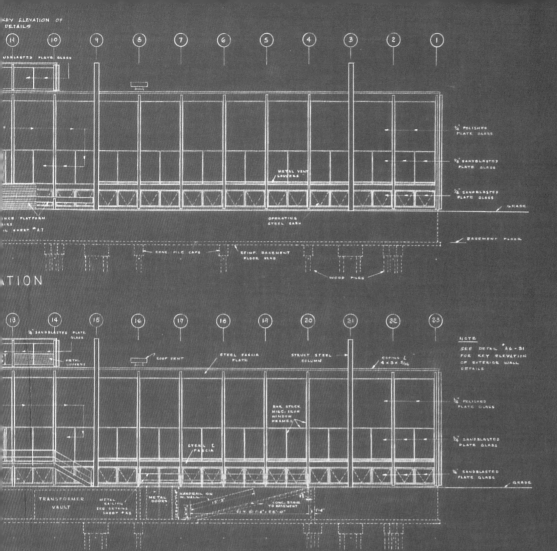

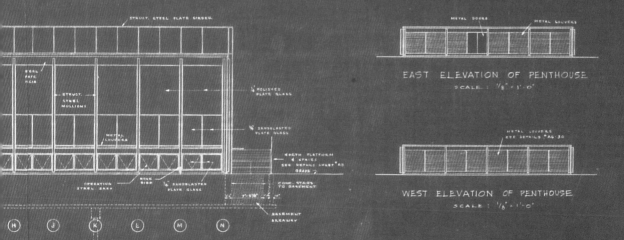

EAST ELEVATION OF PENTHOUSE
SCALE: 1/8" = 1'-0"

WEST ELEVATION OF PENTHOUSE
SCALE: 1/8" = 1'-0"

Since cathedral builders traversed Europe in the Middle Ages, architects have been peripatetic professionals, moving with the shifting demand for their services. The architect and his/her tools traveled together, producing drawings and models wherever they set up shop. Now, the desire for portable tools is often solved by increasingly miniaturized computers powerful enough to run any architectural software. With the Internet and high-speed communications, the architect and his/her information, drawings, and models can travel separately from a device in the architect's hands to another in the hands of the contractor or client a world away. So, now where do we draw the line?

left
"Pretty Neat" drawing board
Dietzgen trade-literature advertisements, mid-twentieth century

opposite
Hewlett-Packard drawing tablet with Revit image displayed in Adobe Acrobat
11 x 8½ x 1 in.

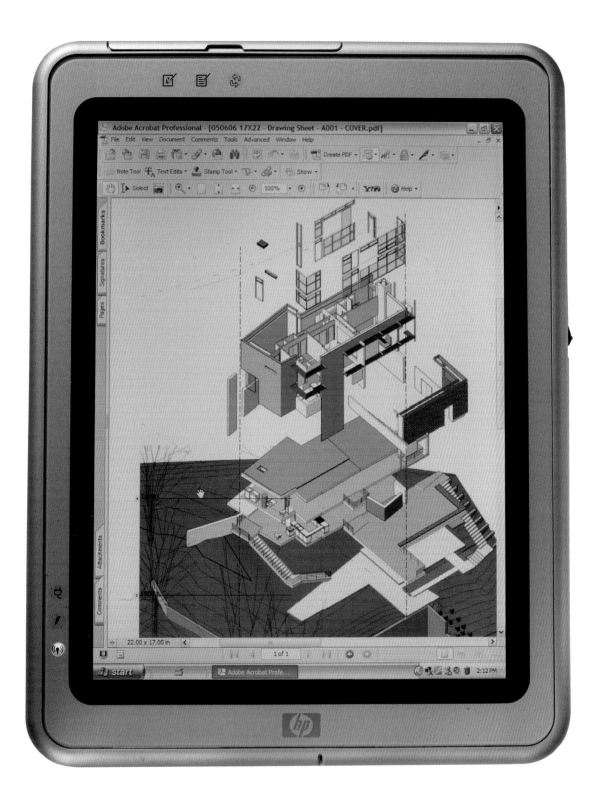

The Lead Pencil: Lever of the Architect's Imagination

Paul Emmons

With over two billion pencils consumed annually in the United States during the twentieth century, pencils are so commonplace that they are easy to overlook. Yet, as a tool of the architect's imagination, the pencil, along with paper, may be the most vital device in architects' attempts to see into the future. As John Robertson, librarian of the London Royal Society, wrote in "A Treatise of such Mathematical Instruments as are usually put into a Portable Case" (1775), "There is not a more useful instrument for ready service in making sketches or finished plans than a black-lead pencil."

Although the computer has become widespread in architectural practices, the image of the architect continues to be closely identified with the simple wood-cased lead pencil. The relationship of the drafter with the pencil is so intimate that it is used metonymically: the architect is a pencil. The American architectural journal *Pencil Points* (1920–1943) began one of its first articles by explaining that the drafter's "pencil should be, in a very real sense, a part of himself, an extension of his hand." The pencil as a tool extending the power of the hand is a common trope. An equally important metaphor for the architect's imagination, although less often acknowledged, is the wood-cased lead pencil as a construction material. Together, the two analogies unite creative sketching on a piece of paper with construction on a building site.

Pencil Stories

In ancient Rome, a pencil was a tiny brush called *penicillus* (little tail)—also the basis for the modern name "penicillin." Beginning in the Renaissance, pencils were called "dry pencils" to distinguish them from brushes. As late as 1843, the *Complete Book of Trades* still found it necessary to announce the change of pencil from a brush to "wood with a groove into which black lead, or *plumago*, a dark shining mineral, is introduced."

It was in the mid-sixteenth century that black lead—what was thought to be lead—was discovered. According to legend, a violent storm overturned a large oak tree in Barrowdale (Cumberland), England, and after the storm passed, local shepherds inspected the hole left by the tree's roots. They discovered a mysterious black substance that proved useful in marking their sheep. This material, too soft to be stone and too hard to be earth, was judged by the Royal Society to be similar to white lead and was thus named "black lead." Barrowdale was the premier source of black lead for over a century and remains the home of the Derwent pencil company. Giovanni Lomazzo's sixteenth-century treatise on art and architecture, *Tratatto dell'arte de la pittura (A Tracte Containing the Artes of Curious Paintinge, Carving and Buildinge)* (1584) recommends it as drawing material, showing that artists quickly adopted black lead for use. In 1620, Sir Roger Pratt described using "black lead Pencils—blackest and least brittle whereof are the best"—for his architectural designs.

Early pencils were merely solid chunks of black lead that were taken from the earth. To make it easier to handle, black lead was wrapped in string or bound into a wooden holder. For example, Henry Peacham's *Art of Drawing* (1607) described as essential "black lead sharpened fine-lie [sic] and put fast into quils." Continuing throughout the eighteenth century, a *porte-crayon* (lead holder) of brass or white metal was in general use. While lead holders were more common, experiments with gluing black lead into wood cases began by the end of the seventeenth century. Friedrich Staedtler, a German carpenter who founded a pencil-making empire, cut black lead into a square and glued it inside two halves of wood in 1662. Many different shapes for the wood casing were employed over the years—square, rectangle, circle, and hexagon, the latter being the most widespread. Triangular wood pencils were promoted to architects because they did not roll off an angled drawing board. Cedar was and remains the preferred wood for pencil casings due to its straight grain, which facilitates even sharpening and gives off a delicious odor during that procedure. Pen knives (used for sharpening quills to apply ink) were used to sharpen pencils well into the twentieth century. Fine emery cloth was also used, and mechanical sharpeners did not appear until the twentieth century.

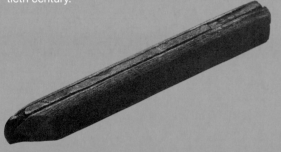

above, top
Sixteenth-century lead pencil

above, bottom
Bundle of drawing pencils
Manufactured by John Thoreau & Co., Concord, Massachusetts, ca. 1840s

opposite
A pointed piece of Wadd wrapped in string

Since the Renaissance, it has been an alchemic belief that black lead named a distinct element of the earth. This conception was upset in 1779 when Swedish chemist Carle Scheele determined that black lead was actually a form of carbon that we now call graphite. In the 1851 Great Exhibition at the Crystal Palace in London, Barrowdale black lead was displayed beside the Koh-i-Noor (mountain of light) diamond because they were both known to consist of carbon. Koh-i-Noor was then adopted as a brand name for a pencil still made today. In 1795, shortly after pencil lead was identified as graphite, France, again at war with England, could not obtain the high-quality Barrowdale writing material. To mitigate the shortage, chemist Nicolas-Jacques Conté patented a process, still used today, to make pencil leads—though precise recipes remain secret. He purified coarse graphite that was locally available by sifting it and mixing the result with clay and water; he then kneaded it and baked the paste into pencil lead.

The hardness of pencil leads is dependent on the proportion of clay mixed with graphite. Softer leads, which make darker lines, do not contain darker lead; instead, they have less clay and leave more fragments of graphite on the paper. Conté's innovation allowed precise calibrations of pencil leads into ranges of B (soft) and H (hard). John Ruskin, the famous nineteenth-century artist and critic, in a book called the *Ethics of Dust* (1866), mused that if the graphite of a pencil crystallized into diamond, it would be HHH. The history of pencils, especially the misconception that they are black lead, continues to influence us today.

Constructing Drawings and Constructing Buildings
Following the introduction of paper making to the West from China during the Renaissance, the beginnings of modern architectural drawing appeared shortly thereafter

in Italy. As today's leading theorist on architectural representation Marco Frascari revealed, paper, a sturdy yet inexpensive drawing support, allowed leading Renaissance architects such as Leon Battista Alberti to practice architecture, for the first time, away from the building site at the drawing board. Thus, early architectural drawings developed from and represented the procedures of on-site building construction. For example, construction lines in drawings simulate the pulling of ropes on site, dimension lines imitate staffs with tied ropes, and centerlines stand for plumb lines. Over the centuries, these drawing techniques slowly became conventionalized as self-referential drawing symbols. As architectural drawings become mere diagrams, their connection to constructing buildings has been lost.

The making of architectural drawings best translates to the construction of buildings not as simulation but as an analogous representation provoking possibilities in the interpreter's imagination. As drawing material represents building material, the challenge for the pencil is to engage the material imagination of the architect despite being removed from the construction site.

Black-lead Material Imagination
While we have known for more than two hundred years that black lead is actually graphite, we still call it a lead pencil. The continuity of the name "lead pencil" demonstrates

that material intuition can be more subtly pervasive in our everyday world than scientific knowledge. Folk beliefs, deriving from actual experience with things, informs our perceptions even when they are in conflict with scientific knowledge. Parents still need reassurance that their children cannot suffer lead poisoning from graphite pencils.

In drawing, pencil lead seems almost immaterial, especially when compared to its more robust siblings, such as ink. The insubstantiality of pencil lines explains, somewhat, its use for preliminary, or "field," drawing and studies. This is in part because during the Enlightenment, black lead was much easier to use on horseback than juggling a quill pen, pen knife, and ink without its spilling. Peacham in 1606 recommended the use of black lead in quills "for your rude and first draught" and Robertson in the next century wrote that the "black-lead pencil is useful to describe the first draught of a drawing, before it is marked with ink; because any false strokes, or superfluous lines, may be rubb'd out with a handkerchief or a piece of bread." Today's manuals of architectural delineation continue to describe the same use of pencils. Geometers since Euclid have conceived their diagrams as immaterial like the breadthless lines they represent. Architectural drawings often allow the same idea of immateriality to be projected upon pencil lines while remaining entities. Even the most advanced scientific pencils using nanotechnology, which can draw lines just one molecule wide, have a material presence, though it is invisible to the naked eye. Although transient, the lead of pencils offers a particular materiality through which it is possible to project the materiality of building construction.

Transmutation of Black Lead into Building Material
The pressure of pencil against paper transforms white into black through the volition of the human hand. The pencil

line drawing a ground plan on paper creates a furrow in the earth, the planting of graphite pollen, seeds of ideas to be harvested during construction. Poet of material images and philosopher of science Gaston Bachelard noted that we say a pencil touches the paper when it is one ten-thousandth of a millimeter from the paper. *Pencil Points* advised the draftsman to "acquire an acute sense of the feel of his pencil on the paper, a delicacy of touch that is not unlike that of the skilled surgeon who is said to be able to almost 'see' with his fingertips." The lead should "bite into the paper" just enough to take hold, neither "digging into the paper [nor] loosely riding over the surface." The pencil's cedar wood acts as a scaffold for the soft lead, to be consumed during construction. Working between internal and external senses, the pencil brings forth images of architecture. It is the resistance felt by the hand between lead and paper that gives drawings depth. Bachelard suggested that in the dynamic reveries of our contact with matter, each touch creates a new substance, and materials touch us as we touch them.

The physical experience of marking pencil on paper becomes the basis for imagining possibilities for building through drawing. Drawing a plan, architect Cesare Cesariano suggested in 1521, is like walking through fresh snow on the building site. The small movements of the architect constructing drawings are analogous to the large movements of the mason constructing buildings. While differing in scale, these two procedures both make the artificers aware of their effort against material resistance. Perhaps the best example of building with a pencil is architect Louis Kahn's admonition to architects, in a writing called "On Stopping Our Pencils." We must, he advises, "train ourselves to draw as we build, from the bottom up, when we do, stopping our pencil to make a mark at the

joints of pouring or erecting [because] in architecture, as in all art, the artist instinctively keeps the marks which reveal how a thing was done." In "On Drawing," Kahn emphasized the importance of material imagination over empirical knowledge: "An architect would draw a tree as he imagined it grew because he thinks of constructing. . . . The architect draws to build." Architects should use their pencils to foresee future constructions.

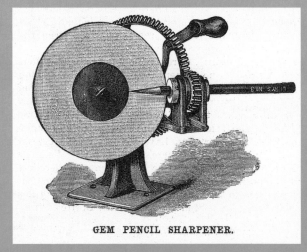

GEM PENCIL SHARPENER.

The Gem, an early mechanical pencil sharpener with sandpaper disk manufactured by Messrs. Gould & Cook for Messrs. Goodnow & Wightman, Boston, Massachusetts.

All great architects of the pencil found techniques for working building materials from how they worked their pencil lead. This was certainly true for early twentieth-century architecture, even from widely different stylistic traditions. Architect Louis Sullivan, himself a "master pencil," used black marks as seeds planted in the vibrant whiteness of paper that corresponded to his view of the vital life of nature inspired by American Transcendentalists like Henry David Thoreau and Walt Whitman. Sullivan's drawings in *A System of Architectural Ornament According with a Philosophy of Man's Powers* (1924) moved from line to point as the "inorganic became organic, the ideal real, and the subjective objective." Published in a way that failed to reproduce the character of his pencil marks, Sullivan complained that the plates appeared "dull and dead rather than alive and breathing in their own atmosphere." The contrasting black and white spots of his pencil drawings translate into the shadows and highlights of the glazed terra-cotta ornament of his buildings. Sullivan utilized extensive undercutting for his terra-cotta designs, requiring workmen to chisel away underpieces of the ornament after the terra-cotta was fired and removed from molds, which resulted in greater contrasts between the glistening light and dark shadowy portions of the ornament. Sullivan's chiseled pencil marks on the drawing paper were translated into the craftsmen's chiseling of the terra-cotta.

Another architect of the pencil and a contemporary of Sullivan, devout Neogothicist Ralph Adams Cram drew thick, broken lines to project the incarnation of his granite collegiate Gothic buildings. His procedure of making broken lines with the pencil evoked the procedure that produced the granite for the building. Large blocks were first quarried and finely finished, only later to be beaten by workmen with chains to break off corners and instantaneously age

the new stones to impart the authority of the old stones of Oxford and Cambridge universities. Cram's Graduate College building at Princeton University was praised at its opening in 1914 as "instant antiquity [where] one has forgotten how entirely new it is." The relation between architect and builder is neither precise nor deterministic but representational. Cram's hand holding the pencil to draw broken lines translated into the workmen's physical use of chains to deteriorate the stone.

The aforementioned architects found material characteristics in their pencil marks that drew them into the metaphysics of their architecture and projected them forward into the physics of their buildings. As architect Adolf Loos wrote in "Architecture" (1930), "from the elevation of a building, from the manner of a piece of ornamentation, one can tell whether the architect was using a no. 1 or a no. 6 pencil." Care in drawing translates into care for building as small gestures transform into large. Architects should become alchemists who transform pencil lead into architectural gold.

The Challenge of Digital Materiality
Since the physical aspects of building are best grasped through the materiality of the architectural drawing, how can computer-generated drawings encourage connection? In computer drawing, the digits of the hand no longer have tactile connection to the production of the drawing; touching keys is physically unrelated to the images that appear on the screen. The goal of most computer rendering is a perfect visual simulacrum of a future building so that the image is entirely lifelike. However, visual realism is not coincident with physical presence. Philosopher George Berkeley, in "Essay Towards a New Theory of Vision" (1709), persuasively argued that visual appearances are signs in

THE INORGANIC:
MANIPULATION OF FORMS IN PLANE-GEOMETRY
MOBILE GEOMETRY

Basic Elemental Forms : shown inscribed in circle.

These simple forms, of ancient discovery and use, were given esoteric meaning and occult powers by the men of that day, in an effort to control, by means of formulas and secret ritual, the destiny of MAN amidst the powers of NATURE. With mystic numbers, and other phenomena, they formed part of an elaborate system of MAGIC : to which the world pinned its FAITH

PLATE
3

Diagram of : CIRCLE
with inscribed regular POLYGONS
The circle is assumed to be the PRIMAL
FORM.

Here however a NEW FAITH is advanced: a faith in MAN : an unwavering faith that MAN, with his natural powers, developed and FREE, may and shall control his DESTINY through the inner magic of his enlarged vision, and of his will to ATTAIN. Master of the Inorganic and the Organic, he will, when he has FOUND himself, become MASTER OF HIMSELF. (See the PRELUDE to this work.)

TECHNICALLY, as an item in the progress of our Demonstration, the above forms, rigid in their quality, are to be considered, in our Philosophy, as CONTAINERS of radial energy : extensive and intensive. Thalatosuv: Extension of form along lines or axes radiating from the center and/or Intention of form along the same or other radials from the Periphery toward the Center. Here then appears the WILL of MAN to cause the Inorganic and Rigid to become FLUENT, through his powers.
Note also that we assume energy to be resident in the PERIPHERY, and that all lines are Energy-lines.
This may be called "PLASTIC GEOMETRY".

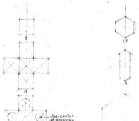

Radial expansion of the SQUARE   Morphology of the HEXAGON

Geometrical extension and intention conserve the idea of AXES. MORPHOLOGY is a process whereby an original form gradually changes into ANOTHER form.

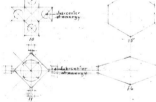

One example of plastic development of equilateral triangle
MORE SUB-AXES IN 20
The sub-centers of energy may extend outward and inward indefinitely
SUB-AXES MAY BE USED AT WILL

Fewer realmen of the Hexagon than shown above for the triangle.
OUR FORMS ARE GRADUALLY BECOMING MOBILE and the sub-axes and the sub-centers of energy are coming into view.

AW 1922

the mind and not identical to the objects themselves. A materially suggestive drawing that invites the viewer's imagination of a future building is a more real representation, in this sense, than that which merely looks alike.

Notions of tools as extensions of the hand have been usurped by contemporary conditions of "abstract machines" that absorb both human and instrument into larger functional systems. Systems such as computer drawing programs threaten to eliminate the material imagination in their production of simulacra. Since computer-aided designers know only through sight, not through touch, they cannot understand the differences between the visual and the physical world and project between them. In the words of philosopher Charles S. Peirce, the indexical relation of drawing and building through physical connection now becomes a symbol that can only be learned through training.

Representational tools that are produced to seemingly fit their specific function precisely make material creation seem unmediated. Friction between a material and its use increases our awareness of its potential physical properties. The analogical thinking between drawing and building was clearer in early times when drawing supplies were collected from various settings such as the kitchen, pharmacy, drawing table, and construction site. For example, in the Renaissance, powered black lead was mixed with white wine as medicine to treat artists and philosophers' affliction of melancholia, associated with emanations from Saturn, the lead planet. Unexpected relationships between materials, like the tradition of using bread for erasure of pencil marks, make us aware of constructional potentialities in a way that single-purpose industrial products do not.

This essay is not advocating technological regression. However, it proposes drawing on over five hundred years of learning and experimenting with the technology of pencils to inform the refinement of our newer and far more complex representational tools, which will determine the nature of our future habitations.

Architectural drawing should be a representational lever to pry open material dreams of possible buildings. In 1930, the modernist architect Le Corbusier recommended that a designer should "acquire the habit of strolling with one's pencil, step by step." It remains commonplace today that, even in this paperless electronic era, a true architect cannot think or talk without a pencil to sketch ideas. Just as the new representational technology of pencil and paper challenged Renaissance architects to rethink the nature of their work away from the construction site, today's new representational technology must find ways to nurture the material imagination.

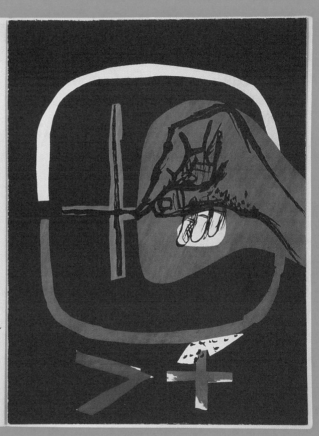

On a
avec un charbon
tracé l'angle droit
le signe
Il est la réponse et le guide
le fait
une réponse
un choix
Il est simple et nu
mais saisissable
Les savants discuteront
de la relativité de sa rigueur
Mais la conscience
en a fait un signe
Il est la reponse et le guide
le fait
ma réponse
mon choix.

150

Avec le carbone nous avons
trace l'angle droit
Reprinted from Le Corbusier,
Poeme de l'angle droit (Paris:
Teriade, 1955).

The Geometry of Art

"For all these things—axes, circles, right angles—are geometrical truths, and give results that our eye can measure and recognize; whereas otherwise there would be only chance, irregularity and capriciousness. Geometry is the language of man." — *Le Corbusier*

Straight lines are the backbone of architectural drawing, but there are many other geometric problems that architects encounter specific to any given building. Conventional tools can solve conventional problems, but the shape of a site, a type of space, or rendering problems can demand the development of a new tool.

The West and East buildings of the National Gallery in Washington, D.C., reveal two interesting drawing problems. The renderings that were drawn for John Russell Pope's West Building show the difficulty of drawing circles in perspective. The arches, vaults, and the rotunda of the West Building all appear as circles in the orthographic drawings, but to depict these elements in perspective, Pope's partner, Otto Eggers, needed to construct ellipses. Knowing the value of a convincing perspective drawing, instrument makers had worked on the problem of accurately portraying ellipses for centuries. A string with two fixed points is sufficient to draw an ellipse, just as a string with one fixed point is sufficient to draw a circle, but architects needed greater precision—something that came with the invention of first the elliptical trammel and later the ellipsograph.

The need for geometric precision was the foundation for the development of special tools required to draw architect I. M. Pei's East Building of the National Gallery, located on a quirky triangular site. The devising of special triangles for the project fell to Yann Weymouth, the chief design architect for the project. Weymouth devoted several pages of his sketchbook to a systematic interrogation of the triangular site, calculating the trigonometry of the angles and proportions. Pei divided the site—one of the peculiar products of L'Enfant's eighteenth-century plan for Washington, D.C.—into two triangles: the primary one an isosceles, its partner a right triangle. No mass-produced triangles suited the angles (19.4731440 and 70.536856 degrees), and adjustable triangles were not sufficiently precise, so Pei had triangles manufactured to suit this particular building. After the construction of the building, these acrylic triangles continued to serve the in-house architecture office of the National Gallery until 1991 when the office made the difficult switch to CAD, first using AES, originally developed by Skidmore, Owings & Merrill (SOM), before shifting to AutoCAD in 1997.

The change from manual to digital has taken a generation, but every architecture practice has undergone it to some degree. This complete shift has consigned many of the older tools to an uneasy fate either as archaic technologies with their own subcultures of users or as obsolete artifacts destined for the dumpster. Technological objects are doomed from the start: in the contemporary world of creative consumption, there is always something newer, better being developed. Historian George Kubler has written in *The Shape of Time* (1962): "The decision to discard something is far from being a simple decision…It is a reversal of values." He continues, speaking more directly of the fate of tools: "Discarding useful things…is more final. A main reason for this pitiless scrapping of the tools of the past is that a tool usually has but one single functional value."

Yet, there is another life for the obsolete object; if it can survive this first reversal of values, it may find itself a valued artifact, under glass in a museum. Most of the East Building triangles have by now been lost or discarded. The computer has essentially ended the era when unique design problems demanded such single-purpose tools.

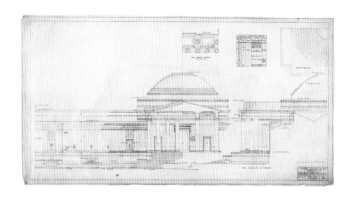

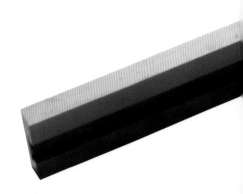

above
National Gallery of Art
West Building drawing #151
(with quarter dome plan)
John Russell Pope, 1938.
Ink on linen, 31¼ x 59 in.

right
Semi-elliptical trammel
William Ford Stanley, ca. 1870.
Brass, steel; 10 x 5 x 1¼ in.

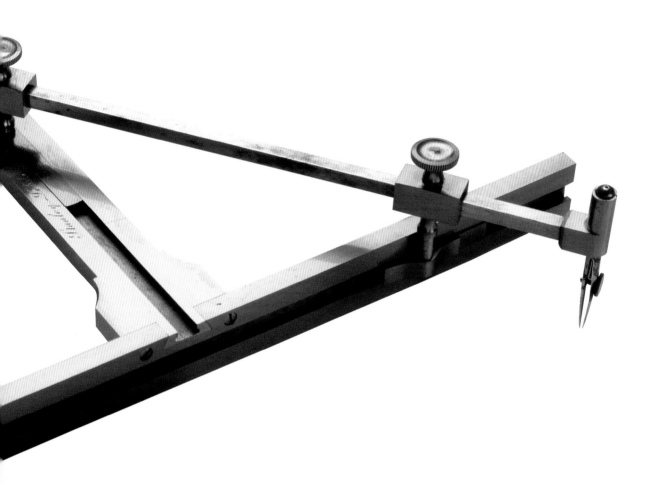

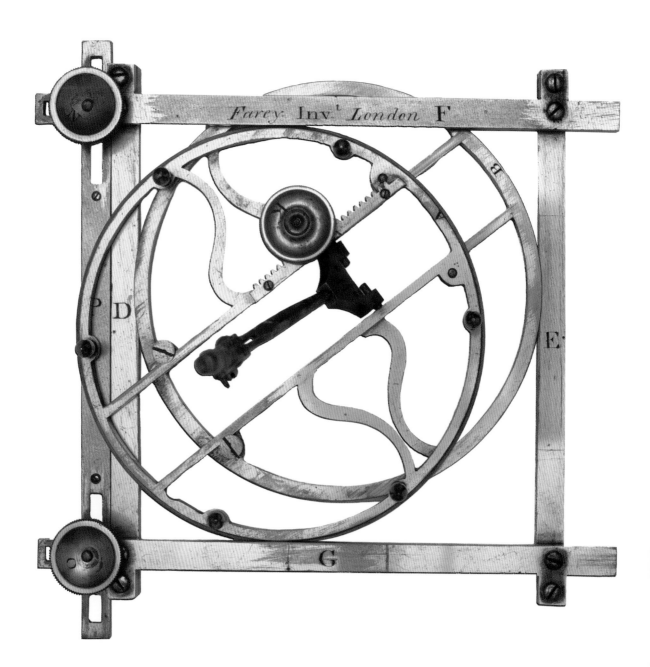

Central Lobby:
Grand Floor, Scheme "D"
John Russell Pope, ca. 1936.
Graphite and gray wash
on paperboard, 10⅞ x 17½ in.

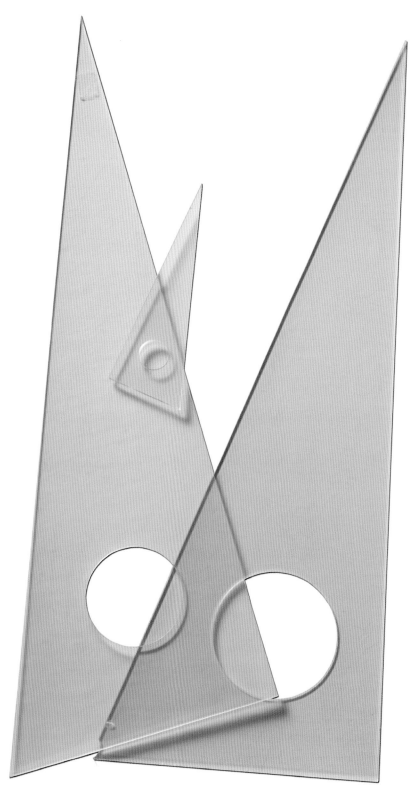

left
**Set squares created for
the design of the National
Gallery of Art East Building,**
ca. 1970. Acrylic, 8 and 12 in.
length, each.

opposite
**Project notebook sketches
for the National Gallery of
Art East Building**
Yann Weymouth, ca. 1970.
Mixed media on paper,
6 x 9 in. each.

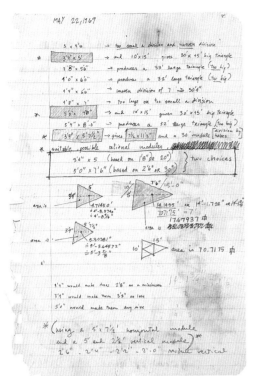

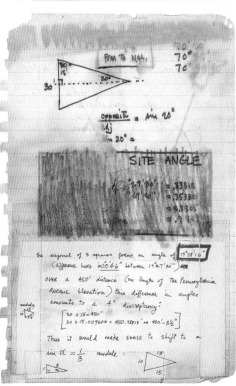

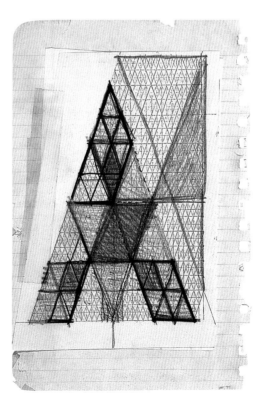

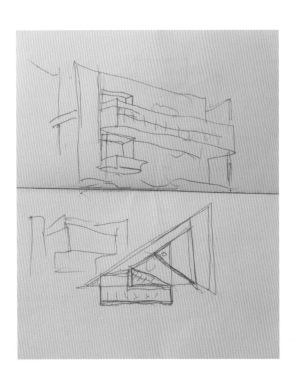

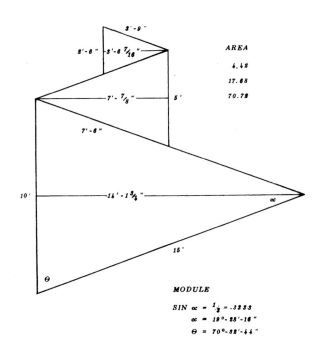

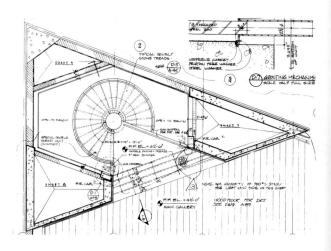

Computing has a history of its own, and we can now look back at what the classic historians would have called its "archaic" phase. The end of the 1960s and the beginning of the 1970s was a time of significant development in computing, but that technology had not yet penetrated the practice of architecture. In 1963, Ivan Sutherland, then a PhD student at MIT, developed a program called Sketchpad, arguably the first computer drawing program. Sutherland wrote in his dissertation: "we have been writing letters to rather than conferring with our computers." Still, making that a meaningful conversation has taken nearly a half century. Sketchpad pioneered the graphical user interface (GUI), which allows interaction with the virtual world without typing in long strings of coded commands. Instead, the user points, clicks, and double-clicks on displays of icons, the virtual tools on the screen.

Light and Shadow

"A great American poet once asked the architect, 'What slice of the sun does your building have? What light enters your room?'—as if to say the sun never knew how great it is until it struck the side of a building." —*Louis Kahn*

In addition to constructing geometries and suites of differentiated lines, the architect needs another type of drawing, and another set of tools, to show what the building will look like once it is realized. Historian James S. Ackerman has referred to these as "rhetorical drawings." Because objects in the real world are caressed by light, the mastery of its representation is crucial to this form of graphic expression. *Sfumato, chiaroscuro,* and *sciagraphy,* the technique of casting and projecting shadows, are some of the delicious words we use to describe the ineffable qualities of light and shadow in drawing and painting.

Painters had held a monopoly on the representation of light and shadow for centuries, but the development of photography in the 1830s raised the standard of verisimilitude. Modernist painters began to focus less on realism and more on the characteristics of light itself, but architectural drafters were still obligated to the portrayal of convincing visions of buildings. The representation of light and shadow depends more on technique than on elaborate tools. The ink wash or water color, used to express the infinite gradations from light to dark, needs nothing more than water, brushes, ink, and color blocks. Building up shadows from finite marks such as hatching and stippling demands nothing more than a handful of sharp pencils and set of technical pens.

Of all the drawing problems in search of tools, the problem of representing light and shadow seems to have the greatest dynamic range from poetry to science. Contemporary architects also use these drawing techniques but are increasingly turning to the computer to render a range of light conditions almost impossible to represent by hand. Surface mapping, ray tracing, and shadow casting can instantly pull a flat drawing into a believable model of reality. Curiously, digital renderings are often hyper-real. Skilled painters and photographers know the importance of atmospheric perspective and depth of field in enhancing their representations, but objects in the CAD-mosphere are always in sharp focus. As with all tools, these tools of instant verisimilitude demand a skilled user.

Today, the representation of light and shadow serves more than an aesthetic purpose. Current software allows architects to represent reflections, artificial and natural daylight, and realistic shadows for any time of the day at any location. Computer programs like Viz can help architects refine where and how sunlight strikes the building to maximize passive solar energy–saving strategies and minimize resource use. Adding variables such as cloud cover and changes to a deciduous landscape can give the architect the tools to tune the building to maximize daylight and thermal comfort and minimize energy consumption. Realistic light and shadows do more than just make striking images: they provide real information for environmentally conscious design. Coupled with programs for mechanical engineers, these light simulations can accurately predict heating and cooling needs. Computer programs that move virtual suns across digital spaces help architects place skylights, arrange windows, size shading elements, even locate trees in the landscape and give them tools they could only dream about in years past.

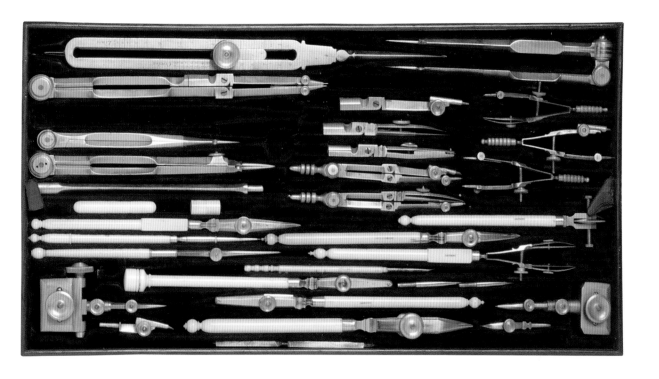

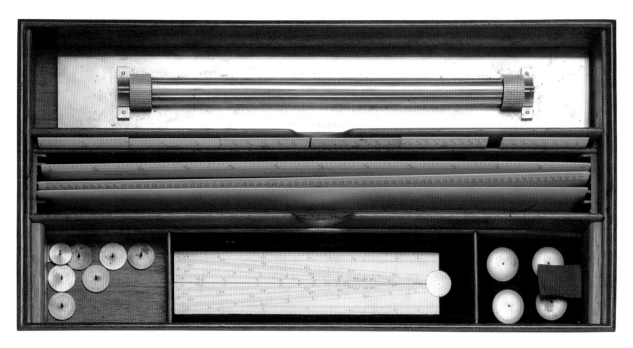

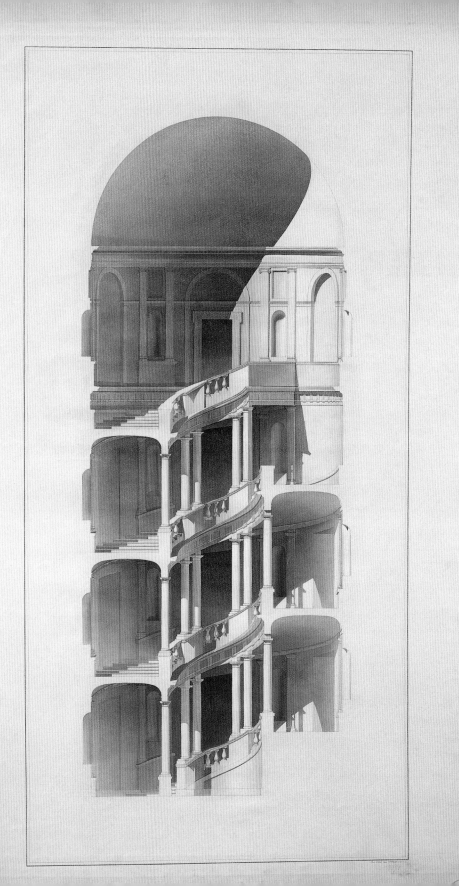

Richard Morris Hunt, the first American architect to be educated at the Ecole de Beaux-Arts in Paris, between 1845 and 1853, learned the techniques of persuasion through sciagraphy and perspective. In addition to passing an entrance exam in drawing, geometry, and history for admittance, once a student, Hunt's course of study at the notoriously competitive Ecole included mastering the techniques of liquid media, such as ink washes and watercolor. His tool set likely contained brushes and dried blocks of ink and pigment for making drawings in the field as well as in the studio. These student drawings demonstrate the talent that made him an acclaimed architect of his generation.

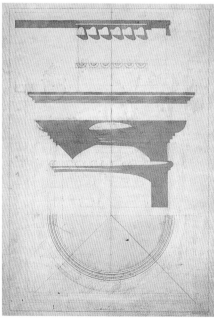

left
Study in Perspective
Richard Morris Hunt Architect, ca. 1845/1846. Ink and wash on paper, 22 x 15¼ in.

right
Theatre of Marcellus
Richard Morris Hunt Architect, 1846. Ink and wash on paper, 25¾ x 19¹/₁₈ in.

opposite
The Five Orders in General
Reprinted from William Salmon, *Palladio Londinensis* (London: S. Biet, 1748), plate IX.

The Five Orders in General

Plate IX

Composite

Corinthian

15 Modules

14 Modules 12 Min

Ionic

13 Mod. 31 M.

12 Mod. 20 M. Doric

10 Mod. 45

Tuscan

Scale of
Minutes

E. Hoppus Delin.

B. Cole Sculp.

below
Digital rendering created with the program Autodesk VIZ
2005

opposite
The Plaza Living Room, Neoscape, Inc.
Digital rendering created with the program Autodesk 3ds Max, 2006

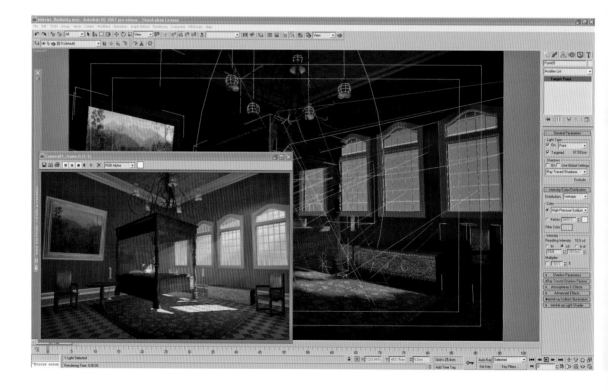

Perspective

"We have enough now on paper to make a perspective drawing to go with the plan for the committee of 'good men and true' to see… a complete building on paper, already." —*Frank Lloyd Wright, An Autobiography, 1932*

The quest for a system for drawing in perspective has been present in both the history of painting and of architecture even before the early fifteenth century, when Italian architect Filippo Brunelleschi developed the theory and method of linear perspective. Drawing in perspective poses a double-sided problem: one is the problem of drawing an accurate perspective of something that already exists, another is of something that exists only in the imagination. Historian Robin Evans has commented in his book *Translations from Drawing to Building* (1997) this latter challenge is what separates architects from traditional artists: architects must draw something that does not yet exist. They cannot rely on observation.

In that sense, the perspective drawings of Frank Lloyd Wright are of an entirely different nature than those by contemporary Mexican architect Mayolo Ramírez Ruíz: the former is literally drawing toward the world; the latter drawing from the world. The tools to make the drawing match the world are equally as complex as the tools to make the world match the drawing: their task is to flatten a three-dimensional world, whether real or imagined, into two dimensions. Ramírez's drawing of the Palacio Nacional is drawn from the world; his goal is to accurately represent the building. He makes detailed perspective drawings the old-fashioned way, intentionally leaving construction marks visible so the viewer can appreciate both the building and the drawing as constructions. Ramírez describes two categories of tools, theoretical and practical, that he employs. The first is the theory of perspective drawing, inherited from the Renaissance; the second includes what he calls *los instrumentos de dibujo architectónico tradicionales* (the traditional tools of architectural drawing): the drawing board, parallel rule, triangles, an HB pencil, and eraser. For large perspectives where the *puntos de fuga* (vanishing points) lie beyond the edge of the paper, Ramírez calls upon a *perspectografo*, which consists of *tres reglas articuladas por un tornillo* (three straight rules articulated by a screw). Ramírez is describing a centrolinead, the device invented by architect Peter Nicholson in 1814.

Over the last century and a half, changes in theories about space and time have eroded the power of the perspective drawing. The same theories in art that led to early modern movements such as cubism and impressionism changed the way architects thought about representing space. Additionally, a photograph could more easily and accurately capture the qualities of a space. Software has magnified that ease and accuracy in representing the illusion of space, while animations and view-bubbles have obliterated the traditional single viewpoint. In digital perspectives, the station point is no longer stationary. The computer command "view_perspective" both masks and relies upon a series of complex instructions in code, but the computer itself follows the instructions, so we do not have to.

left
Perspective glass
late eighteenth century.
Mahogany, glass; 25⅝ x 10½ in.,
base 8⁹⁄₁₆ in. diameter.

opposite
Concours de Perspective,
Vaulted Interior
Richard Morris Hunt Architect,
1847. Ink on paper, 25 x 19⅝ in.

Instrumentos de Dibujo
Mayolo Ramírez Ruíz, Arquitecto

*"Las herramientas prácticas que utilicé para hacer este boceto
son los instrumentos de dibujo arquitectónico tradicionales: mesa
de dibujo (restirador) con lámpara, regla de paralelas, juego de
escuadras de acrílico, papel de calco (mantequilla), lápiz HB (minas
de 0.5 mm.) y goma de borrar. Cuando he realizado una perspectiva cónica de gran formato, he utilizado un 'perspectógrafo,' que
consiste en tres reglas articuladas por un tornillo, y que reemplaza
a los puntos de fuga distantes que suelen quedar fuera de la mesa
de dibujo. El formato pequeño del dibujo que nos ocupa permitió
tener todos los elementos de la perspectiva dentro de la mesa
de dibujo: observador, plano del cuadro, horizonte y puntos de
fuga. En lo personal, para este tipo de bocetos prefiero utilizar el
lápiz debido a la facilidad en su aplicación y al resultado a la vista,
agradable y clásico."*

Drawing Instruments
Mayolo Ramírez Ruíz, Architect

"Talking about the practical tools used in this drawing, there are the
desk, parallel rule, triangle rules, HB pencil, and eraser. These are
the simple tools, but if I draw a conical perspective in a greater
format, I use one called 'perspectografo.' It consists in three rules
articulated by a screw that replaces the leak points in the drawing. It is typical to be outside the paper space anyway. The small
format is easier to draw because all the leak points are positioned
into the desk space and paper space. I prefer to use pencil in
this kind of format because it has a result that can be appreciated
in my personal point of view, as a pleasant and classical style."

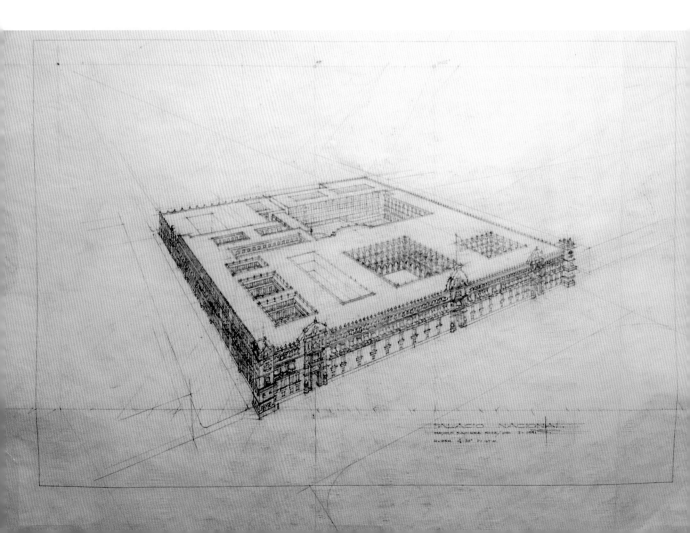

opposite
Palacio Nacional,
Ciudad de Mexico
Mayolo Ramirez Ruiz
Architect, 1990. Pencil
on paper, 17 x 22 in.

right
Perspectograph
Adrien Gavard, ca. 1845.
Brass, steel, ivory;
18¼ x 3¼ x 3 in.

CENTROLINEAD.

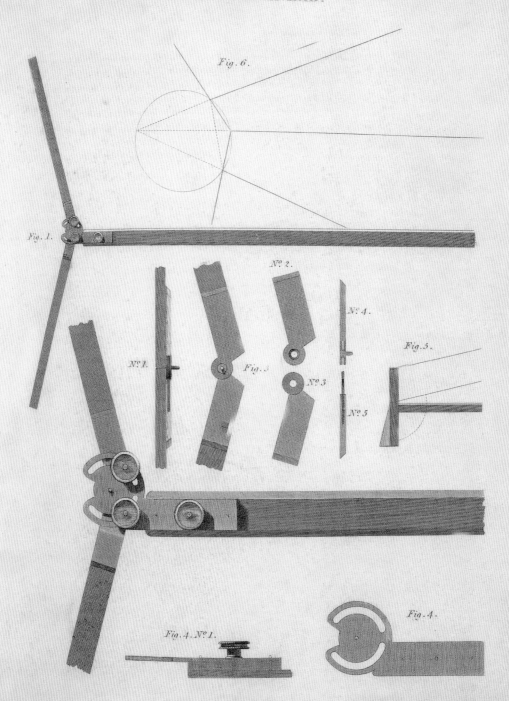

Drawn by M.A.Nicholson.

Engraved by W. Evans.

London, Published by Thos. Kelly, 17 Paternoster Row, Oct.r 1.st 1823.

The instructions instrument-maker Peter Nicholson offers in his book *The New Practical Builder and Workman's Companion* (1825) for setting the centrolinead reads like instructions for building— rather than drawing—a perspective:

"Draw two lines tending to the vanishing point, or to the station point, which must be found by a problem: then put two pins in vertically, over each other, on each side of the line without the space, making the distances on each side of the line nearly the same. Press the two edges of the legs, which run to the center of the joint, against the pins, and move them along till the edge of the blade, which passes through the center of the joint, coincides with the line or crosses it; then loosen the screw that fastens the blade to the leg of the centrolinead, and press the legs gently against the pins till the blade coincides with the line: then fasten that screw, and loosen the other; next move the instrument down to the other line, fasten the screw, and the instrument is set."

opposite
Centrolinead
Reprinted from Peter Nicholson, *The New Practical Builder and Workman's Companion* (London: Thomas Kelly, 1825).

below
Digital rendering created with the program SketchUp
2005

below
Pope-Leighey House: view
Frank Lloyd Wright, ca. 1936.
Pencil on tracing paper,
20⅞ x 36¼ in.

opposite, top
**Frank Lloyd Wright at Work
on Mile High Building**
1956. Gelatin-silver print.
Photograph by OBMA.

opposite, bottom
***Pope-Leighey House: view,
plan, and elevation***
Frank Lloyd Wright, ca. 1936.
Pencil on tracing paper,
20⅞ x 36¼ in.

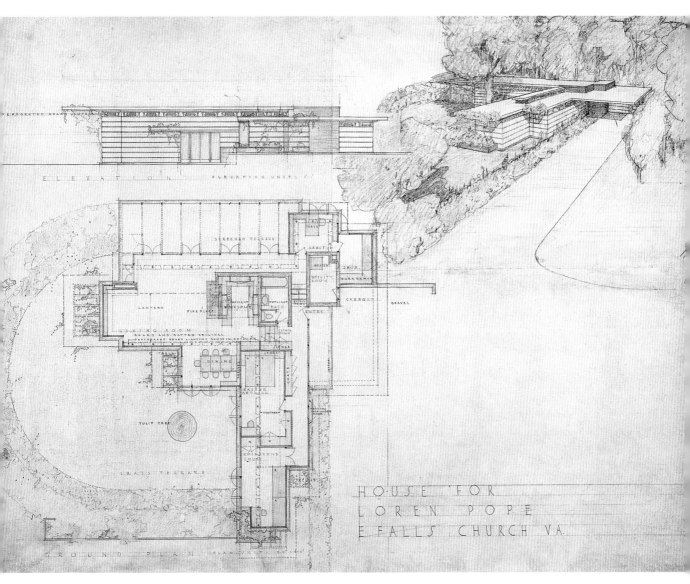

HOUSE FOR
LOREN POPE
E FALLS CHURCH VA.

Design Tools:
A Collector's Perspective and an Architect's Odyssey

David V. Thompson, AIA

Throughout both my collector's and professional journeys into the world of architectural instruments, several common threads have emerged: First, there is great value in understanding the role of historical architectural tools because they challenge the profession to constantly reevaluate the process by which one delivers good design. Second, the simpler, more user-friendly the instrument, the more successful it is, no matter if it is a primitive tool or a modern-day computer modeling program. Finally, much of my interest in antique architectural instruments originates from my personal odyssey as an architect. Not only have I been amazed by the evolution of instruments throughout history, but also over the past fifty years, I have experienced firsthand the remarkable ways in which the advancement of technology and thought in instrument design has changed the profession.

My introduction to drawing tools occurred in sixth grade while I was taking a required drafting class. The evening after the first class, my enthusiastic description of what I had learned inspired my father, an engineer, to uncover a drawing board, T-square, and a chest of instruments—pens and pencils, inks, and linen tracing cloth—from the attic. Already an avid sketcher and painter, I was thrilled to learn this new, precise way of drawing and to add devices to my toolkit. Though it tested my patience at the time—but later beneficial to my interest in collecting—my father encouraged me to draw on linen with a ruling pen and India ink as he had. I soon discovered the pitfalls of incorrectly holding the pen, drawing too-wide lines, and running out of ink mid-line, and I learned to erase unsatisfactory lines with a knife blade. By eighth grade, I was hooked. My heroes became Frank Lloyd Wright and Eero Saarinen, and I had decided to become an architect.

Long before my own journey as an architect began and my interest in architectural tools blossomed, drawing instruments captured the imaginations of ancient civilizations. The history of drawing instruments began with squares and dividers. Instruments of wood and other materials likely existed in the ancient world, but the remaining artifacts are primarily iron and bronze from the Roman period and include scribes, pairs of dividers, squares, and scale rules.

Drawing instruments have always had special meaning to the architect. In portraits of architects, mathematicians, and scientists throughout history, drawing instruments are often pictured alongside them, symbolizing education and knowledge. The tools an architect needs to draw a line or an arc, or to measure and divide, reflect an intermingling of math and art and have changed little from the end of the Dark Ages until the mid-twentieth century. Be it a simple ruling pen, compass, set square, or the most sophisticated computer, the makers of drawing instruments often have been mathematicians and scientists or skilled mechanics and metal smiths. These instruments, handmade and beautifully sculpted and engraved on their surfaces, left a legacy of beauty.

During the Renaissance, the growth of arts and sciences drove a need for these instruments, and artists, scientists, silversmiths, and goldsmiths became the inventors of these tools. Architect Filippo Brunelleschi's quantified perspective in the early 1400s and the science of warfare impacted the technology of instrument making. These events led to the development of early calculating instruments and perspective devices, including tools for drawing ellipses, the shape of a circle in perspective.

The development of scientific instrumentation is directly influenced by the science and technology of the time. In 1597, Galileo modified the military sector to create the Galilean Sector, the first general purpose calculating device and a standard element of instrument sets through the mid-nineteenth century. This was followed in 1625 by mathematician and Anglican minister William Oughtred's invention of the slide rule, a fixture of engineers' and architects' tools into the 1970s.

During the eighteenth century, the development of analytical and descriptive geometry helped introduce new tools for representing complex constructions. The great surge in the construction of bridges, viaducts, and public buildings re-quired drawings with arches, which necessitates an ellipse in nonorthogonal and perspective views. This stimulated a late-eighteenth- and early-nineteenth-century resurgence in the exploration of ellipse-drawing instruments.

At each end of the eighteenth century, seminal books described drawing instruments. The first, *The Construction and Principal Uses of Mathematical Instruments* by Nicolas Bion, the instrument-maker to the French king, Louis XIV, was published in 1709 and first translated to English in 1723 by Edmond Stone. In 1791, George Adams, instrument-maker to King George, wrote *Geometrical and Graphical Essays*. Due to their popularity, both books were reprinted multiple times and were translated into numerous languages. This unified and expanded the impact on the design of future instruments and, ultimately, the arts and sciences. The eighteenth century also saw the invention of instruments specific to architecture, such as the architecto-nic sector and volute compass (also called a helicograph).

With industrialization in full swing in the nineteenth century, scientific and drawing instrument makers transitioned from hand-crafted to machine-made tools to meet increas-ing demand. The mechanization of the tool-production process resulted in the development of several distinct lines of instruments: a student, or low-cost, line entirely machine made; an intermediate line with machine finishing; and a traditional line with hand finishing. Over time, centers of instrument making developed in Italy, Germany, France, and England; corresponding with the expansion of the British Empire, the English dominated the industry from the mid-eighteenth century through the nineteenth century. Individual instrument producers in Austria, the Netherlands, and Switzerland also produced tools.

The first American manufacturers of high-quality instrument technology were Theodore Alteneder in Philadelphia, Pennsylvania, and Keuffel and Esser Co. in Newark, New Jersey. The most notable maker of the period was William Ford Stanley in London, who started his own company

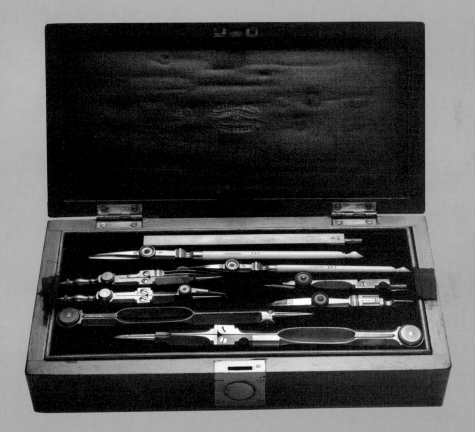

Portrait of Architect
William Buckland (1734–1774)
Charles Willson Peale, Oil on
canvas, 27½ x 36⅝ in.

above
A typical full set
William Ford Stanley, ca. 1900.
Nickel-silver, steel, ivory,
with mahogany case;
7½ x 4¾ x 2 in.

A standard set of drawing tools included a main compass with
interchangeable ink and pencil legs, a divider, a pair of ruling
pens, and a set of bows or spring bows for small circles. A sector,
rectangular protractor/scale rule, and parallel completed the set.
In less-expensive sets, the instruments were made of brass with
boxwood or ebony rules and handles; nickel-silver and ivory were
used in higher-end sets.

Sometimes instruments have a story. The engraving on the silver dedication plate on the lid of this beautiful flame-veneered mahogany case reads, "Presented to H. S. Penn by H. R. H. the Duke of Edinburgh upon the paying off of the *Galatea* 1871." The Duke of Edinburgh at the time was Prince Alfred, who was the son of Queen Victoria. He captained the *Galatea*, one of England's first hybrid steam/sail ships, on a cruise to Sydney, Australia, in 1867. H. S. Penn has been identified as a son of the founder of the company that built the maritime steam engines for the *Galatea*. The set is complete and of the finest quality, produced by Elliott Brothers, one of the leading tool makers of nineteenth-century London.

H. S. Penn presentation set
ca. 1871, manufactured by Elliott Bros., London, England. Nickel-silver, steel, ivory, ebony, pearwood, watercolor blocks, with flame-veneer mahogany case; 16⅝ x 6⅛ x 2 in.

making boxwood curves, scale rules, and set squares. His treatise, "Mathematical Drawing Instruments," first printed in 1866 and reproduced to at least a seventh edition in 1900, is a detailed exposition of nearly every instrument made at the time of printing, their basic construction, and how they were used. Stanley conceived of many new instruments and made significant improvements to many others until the business finally liquidated in 1999. His apprentices went on to found competing companies such as W. H. Harling.

At the onset of the twentieth century, little change had occurred in the basic set of instruments used by the architect other than in the details and materials of construction: stainless steel and plastics replaced brass, nickel-silver, and ivory. Mass production of instruments meant disposal of older tools as technology evolved. With the advent of affordable computer-aided drafting and design systems based on the 1980s personal computer, few survived into the 1990s. Many of these companies attempted to make the transition to computer-aided design—providing plotters and other peripherals to support the digital office—but none were successful.

Hewlett Packard released the first handheld scientific calculator, the HP-35, in 1972. Even with a price of more than $400, the ability to perform continuous calculations, including trigonometric and exponential functions, spurred competitors to create a wide range of ceaselessly improving calculators and relegated the slide rule to historic artifact. When I entered college in 1968, all architecture and engineering students were expected to have a slide rule and take a class on its use. By my first semester of graduate school, the calculator was an indispensable tool for both students and professors.

Like the development of manual drawing instruments, a period of free-for-all experimentation by a large number of software developers occurred. In the new age of accelerating computer speeds and capabilities, the entire life cycle of technological innovation had been shortened from centuries to years, bringing the end of traditional drawing instruments. By the late 1990s, modeling, rendering, and animation software was maturing and had become affordable. Computer-aided design (CAD) software became the standard format for delivering working drawings, embraced especially by the younger generation of architects, who were spending far too much time mastering the intricacies of CAD instead of mastering architecture. As the increase in complexity of an instrument often deters from its use, computers and software that are intuitive, easy to use, and meet day-to-day needs are often the most rapidly adopted.

My odyssey came full circle in 1996 when a close friend presented me with a copy of Maya Hambly's book *Drawing Instruments 1550–1980* (1988). An expansion of the catalog for an exhibit held by the Royal Institute of British Architects in 1982—the last exhibition of its kind until TOOLS OF THE IMAGINATION —it made me want to learn more about these beautiful and largely unknown instruments. In particular, a photograph of an 1813 Farey ellipsograph transformed my curiosity into a desire to search out the oddities of my predecessors.

The continued study of architectural instruments of the past provides great opportunities for today's architects to understand the best practices that have endured throughout history and emphasizes the important lessons of previous generations.

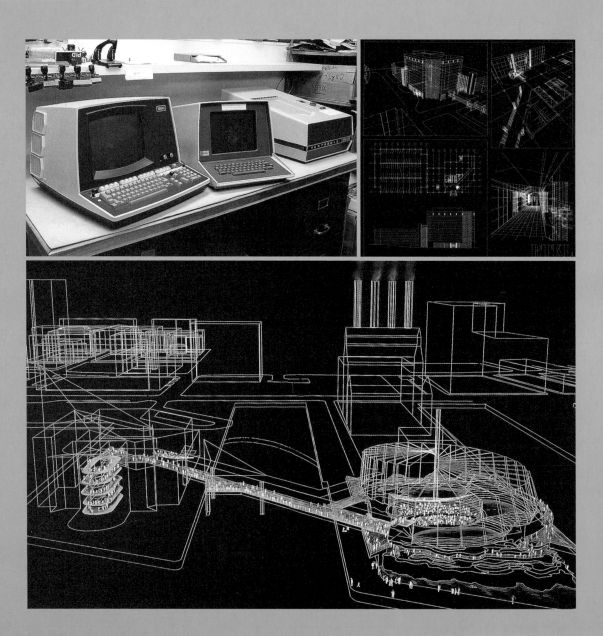

opposite, top left
Computers
ca. 1980

opposite, top right and bottom
**Computer and wireframe
CADD graphics**
ca. 1980

above
**An extracted sectioned
perspective generated from
a Revit model**
ca. 2005

Copying

"This is what the machine may do for us, place beauty for us in many places where otherwise it may be in only one. The artist creates and the machine tool enriches the lives of the individuals." —*Louis Gibson*

Though well armed with tools of precision and tools of persuasion, architects also need the tools for copying, translating, disseminating, saving, and changing the information necessary to make the building. Constructing a building involves a large cast of characters, each needing the same information. The dissemination of accurate copies has been a problem for architects throughout history, magnified in the nineteenth century by the increased scale of architectural projects—larger buildings, like skyscrapers and railway terminals, involve larger and more specialized work crews.

In traditional art and architectural education, copying was a means of education for students. Architect Louis Sullivan believed that learning from nature was more important than learning from tradition. He was, like many of his contemporaries, interested in the search for architectural ornament within the forms of nature and was committed to drawing—copying—nature carefully by hand. He warns in his essay "Young Man in Architecture": "The mind will inevitably reproduce what it feeds upon. If it feeds upon dust, it will reproduce dust. If it feeds upon nature, it will reproduce nature." Only by actively sketching and reproducing the forms of nature could the architect hope to understand them.

Copying to learn and copying to disseminate are two very different tasks, and the latter demands more speed and accuracy than the hand may be able to offer. The printing press solved some of that problem but could only reproduce at the same size as the original. The pantograph, developed in 1603, provided mechanical assistance to the hand in enlarging or reducing. It was particularly useful for reproducing land surveys where the curving lines and idiosyncrasies of natural features were essential. By 1900,

it was on the verge of obsolescence as the new technology of blueprinting became the preferred tool of reproduction (though the pantograph could still be ordered from W. F. Stanley's catalog in 1960). The blueprint, with its characteristic white lines on a blue background, was itself eclipsed by the more easily read diazo print, with blue lines on a white background. Although one is a negative image and the other positive, both are chemically processed contact prints. The large digitizing tables common in architects' offices during the transition from hand drawing to CAD worked on a similar principle as the pantograph but with the objective of making an electronic file from a physical drawing. The generation of architects who served their internships feeding photosensitive paper into the diazo machine, then presided over the next generation of interns hunched over a digitizer tracing, clicking, and copying a drawing by virtually lifting the lines from the paper on which they had been drawn. Today, however, making multiple copies of drawings and documents is so simple that we hardly think about it.

Technology leads and society ambles a few paces behind. Photographer William Henry Fox Talbot's photographic explorations revolutionized seeing, but they also had an unforeseen side effect: photographic reproduction undermined the authority of the original. In his essay "The Work of Art in the Age of Mechanical Reproduction," Walter Benjamin posed the question of the relationship between an original and its copies. Its logical sequel, the work of art in the age of digital reproduction, has yet to be written, but the question is firmly embedded in every aspect of contemporary culture. Now there is no "original" drawing, only a digital file from which innumerable identical prints can be made. Are they all copies? Or are they all originals?

right
**Stanley's improved
pantograph**
William Ford Stanley, ca. 1900.
Brass, ivory casters; 27 x 7½ x
4½ in.

below
Pantograph
Reprinted from Adams,
*Geometrical and Graphical
Essays,* 3rd ed., plate XXXI.

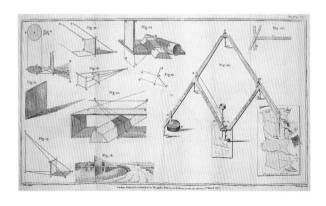

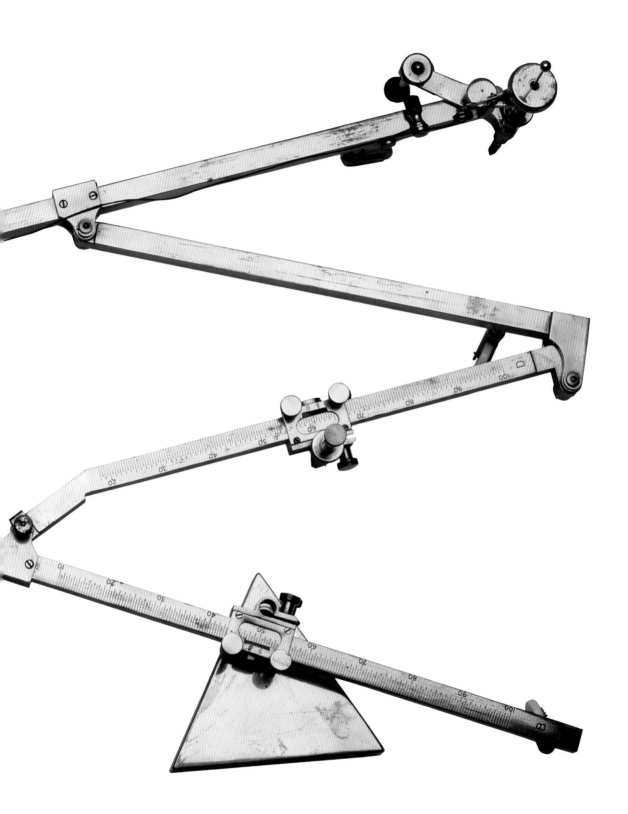

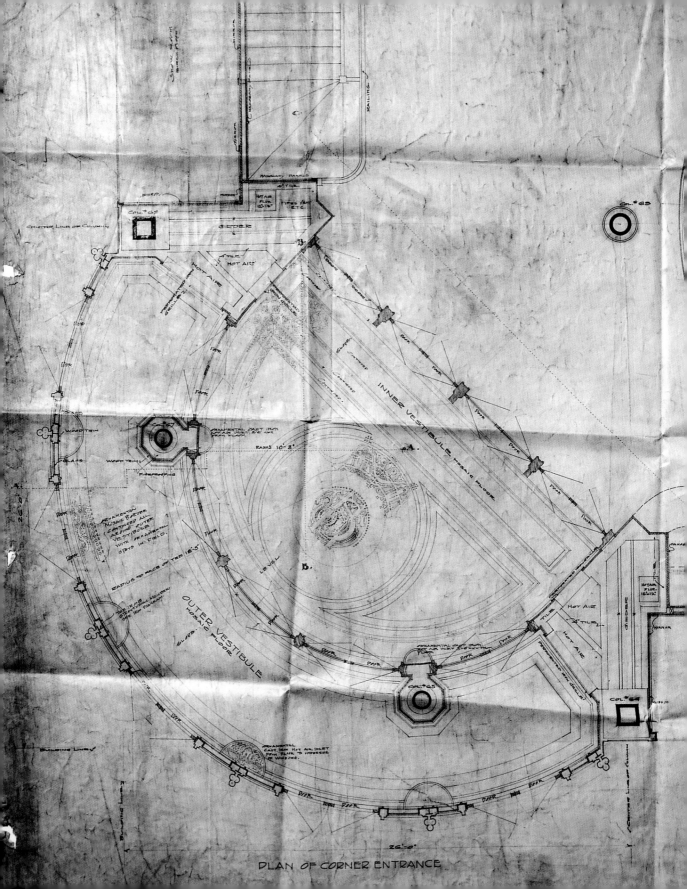

PLAN OF CORNER ENTRANCE

Architect Louis Sullivan embraced the power that industrialization brought to the tools of drawing as well as to building itself. His ornamental motifs, for example, could, as a result, be easily reproduced through casting. Unfortunately, only a few of Sullivan's original drawings still survive. This section dedicated to the tools of copying is, itself, composed mostly of copies, and copies of copies: digitized enlargements of photographs of hand drawings and digitized copies of blueprints, themselves photochemical copies of hand drawings.

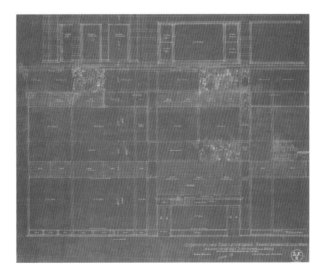

opposite
Floor plan of the corner entrance vestibules, Schlesinger & Mayer building, Chicago, Illinois.
Louis Sullivan, undated.
Pencil on paper.

right
Elevation of lower stories at northwest corner showing ornamental ironwork, Schlesinger & Mayer building,
Louis Sullivan, 1898.
Blueprint, 40½ x 30 in.

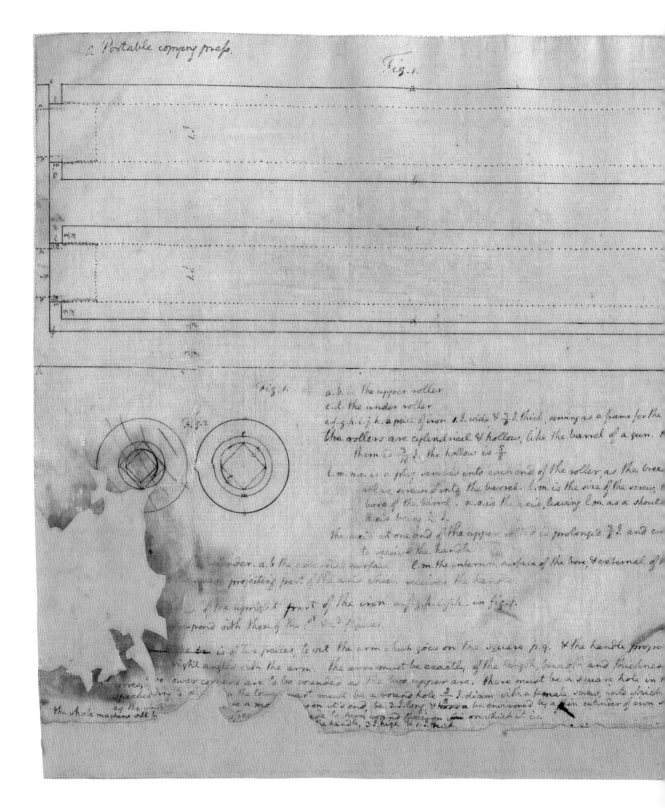

A Portable copying press.

Fig. 1.

Fig. 1.

Fig. 2.

a.b. the upper roller
c.d. the under roller
e.f.g.h.i.j.k. a peice of iron s.I. wide & ⅞ I. thick, serving as a frame for the
the rollers are cylindrical & hollow, like the barrel of a gun.
them is 3/16 I. the hollow is ⅝
l.m. n.o. is a plug screwed into each end of the roller, as the breech
          ... is screwed into the barrel. l.m. is the size of the screw, t
          bore of the barrel. n.o. is the axis, leaving l.m. as a shoulder
          axis being s.l.
the axis at one end of the upper roller is prolonged ⅞ I. and cut
          to receive the handle.
          ...inder. a.b the external surface l.m. the internal surface of the bore, & external of t
          square projecting part of the axis which receives the handle.
          of the upright part of the iron a.f.g.h.i.j.k. in fig.1.
          ...pond with those of the 1st & 2d figures
          ...ta... is of two peices to cut the arm which goes on the square p.q. & the handle projec
          right angles with the arm. the arm must be exactly of the length, breadth and thickness
          ...lower corners are to be rounded as the two upper are. there must be a square hole in t
          ...in the long part must be a round hole 5/... I. diam with a female screw into which
          ...re a m... ...on it's end, be 3.I. long & ... a tin environed by a tin cylinder of iron...
the whole machine will be ... ...e to turn ... ... on which it is.
          ...e handle, 3 I. high & 1. I. thick

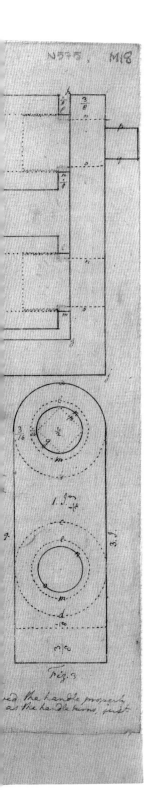

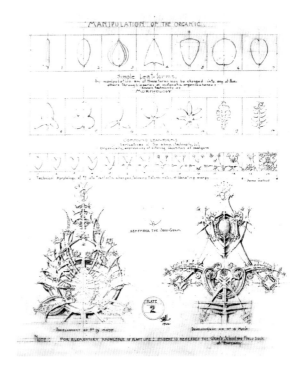

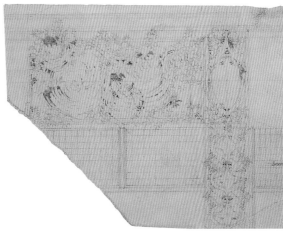

left

Portable copying press
Thomas Jefferson, undated.
Ink on paper, 7¹⁵/₁₆ x 9³/₁₆ in.

right, top

**System of Architectural
Ornament According with a
Philosophy of Man's Powers:
Manipulation of the Organic**
Louis Sullivan, 1922. Pencil on
paper, 57½ x 73½ cm.

right, bottom

**Pencil study for cast-iron
spandrel, Schlesinger &
Mayer building**
Louis Sullivan, ca. 1898

From Model to Drawing to Building

The purpose of all design representations, but of models in particular, is to narrow the distance between an idea and reality, between the images and representations of what we hope the building to be and what it eventually will be. Design is miniature construction, an attempt to model a possible world and make predictions about it and its future conjugation with the existing world.

Drawing as a means of visualizing is a relatively recent addition to the architect's arsenal. As late as the Renaissance, architects were producing large models, usually of wood, to help their patrons understand the projects they were funding. Paper was relatively scarce until the fifteenth century and tracing paper was not common until the eighteenth century, but wood, plaster, and clay were available materials and could easily make models as buildings. While the tools for building models are analogous to tools of construction, many architect's tools are devoted to translating a three-dimensional image in the mind to a two-dimensional sheet of paper and then back into a three-dimensional building—in essence, flattening the world in order to remake it.

If technology is always a step ahead of society, creativity is always one step ahead of technology. By the late 1980s, architect Frank Gehry, a devoted model maker, had realized that his tools could not keep pace with his imagination. Curiously, it was not the efficiency of digital technologies that attracted Gehry to the computer but the power of visualizing and representing things too difficult, or impossible, to do by hand. The hand, however, is where the process begins. While his design intentions have always been expressed with scribbles, crumpled paper, and clay—whatever is close at hand—translating those intentions into a set of instructions for a building had become almost impossible in the conventions of architectural drawing. Gehry and his team decided to look outside of the discipline of architecture for tools to help represent the complex curves and relationships they were exploring. Their search led them to redefine the nature of a model and the relationship between drawing and modeling.

During the design process, colored wood blocks, scraps of fabric, sandwich wrappers, three-dimensional digitizers borrowed from the medical profession, and CATIA, the complex software program developed for the automotive and aerospace industry, are all pressed into service to give form to Gehry's imagination.

Ultimately, two types of models, physical and digital, share authority for the translation of Gehry Partners' final design into construction documents, the traditional set of instructions in drawings and words that describe the final building. The large physical model serves as record of the design process, and the CATIA model is the source of the information for the construction drawings. The contract documents both refer to and are derived from the CATIA model, but CATIA is not CAD. It belongs instead to the family of software referred to as building information modeling (BIM) software that challenges the very definitions of "model" and "drawing." Because its uses the same basic hardware as CAD systems, BIM might appear to be an evolution of CAD, but appearances can be deceiving. BIM is a revolution.

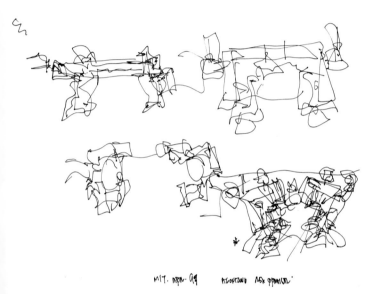

above and opposite, top
**Design sketches, Ray &
Maria Stata Center,
Massachusetts Institute
of Technology (MIT),
Cambridge, Massachusetts.**
Frank O. Gehry, 1999. Ink on
paper, 9 x 12 in. each.

opposite, bottom
**Programming model, Ray &
Maria Stata Center, MIT**
Gehry Partners, 1999.
Painted wood, 22¾ x 16 x 3 in.

following page
**Design process model, Ray
& Maria Stata Center, MIT**
Gehry Partners, 1999. Wood,
foam core, Plexiglas, paper;
29¾ x 26¾ in.

following page, inset
**Production of final
design model, Ray & Maria
Stata Center, MIT**
Gehry Partners, 2000

MIT. DEZ.98

MIT. 99

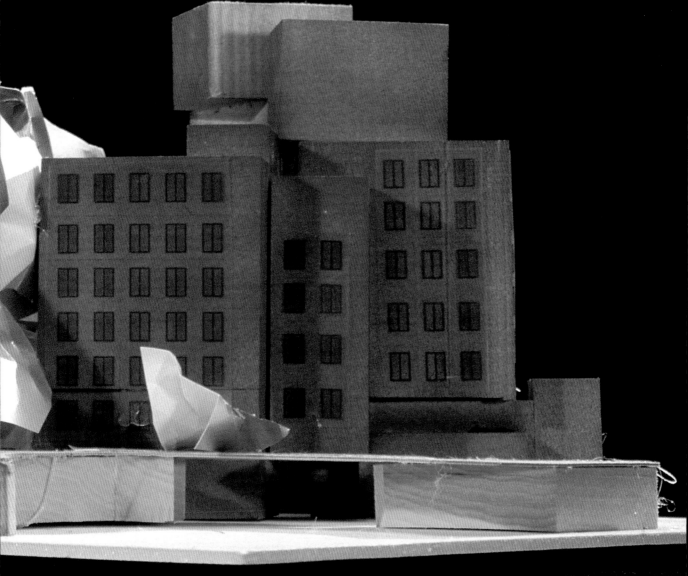

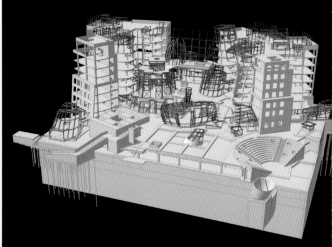

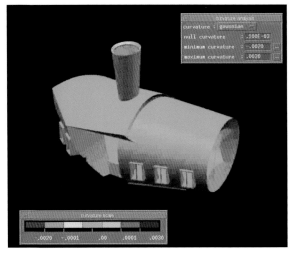

opposite, clockwise from top left

Concrete structure CATIA model, concrete structure with structural-steel CATIA model, and exterior CATIA master geometry, Ray & Maria Stata Center, MIT
Gehry Partners, 1999

right, top

"The Nose" with panel layout in building context, Ray & Maria Stata Center, MIT
Gehry Partners, 1999

right, center

First & second floor plan, Ray & Maria Stata Center, MIT
Gehry Partners, 1999

right, bottom

Gaussian curvature analysis CATIA model for "The Nose," Ray & Maria Stata Center, MIT
Gehry Partners, 1999

"Stale crumb of bread is better, if you are making a delicate drawing, than India-rubber, for it disturbs the surface of the paper less: but it crumbles about the room and makes a mess; and, besides, you waste the good bread, which is wrong." —John Ruskin

The digital world is all about second chances. Even the most casual computer user has become accustomed to being able to undo, backspace, and even retrieve things from the recycle bin, all with a keystroke or two. The simple undo and redo actions are at the root of all computer commands pertaining to modifications, but architects had been correcting and reconsidering for a long time before the undo and redo commands ever appeared on a computer screen. When paper was scarce and expensive, the technology of erasing was laborious: a sharp knife was used to scrape off the ink and bread crumbs were used to grind away graphite. Scientist and inventor Joseph Priestley, better known for identifying the element oxygen, discovered in 1767 that rubber could be used as an eraser. By the mid-twentieth century, architects could choose from a buffet of erasers, including the familiar chunks of pink or white, various blobs of kneaded gray, and a few long, skinny tubes for use in an electric eraser. With chemically impregnated chucks in an electric eraser and a thin metal eraser shield, an architect had a correction tool to match the efficiency of technical pens.

Drawing quickly and precisely, and erasing and redrawing with equal velocity, architects were reaching the limits of speed in the production of hand drawings. But there was still a direct relationship between the time it took to lay down a line and the time it took to remove it. The easy and invisible elimination granted by the delete button on the computer changed that equation forever. But the progress of a design—so important to historians and architects—revealed in successive versions of a project, is lost. Billie

Tsien, of Tod Williams Billie Tsien Architects (TWBTA), warns that trouble can hide in a computer drawing. The clean screen never shows the distress that paper shows when it has been scraped, erased, and drawn over. Borrowing a tool more common to precomputer office work, TWBTA regularly uses correction fluid not so much to erase elements but to draw attention to the areas that need work.

The TX-2 computer that Ph.D. candidate and engineer Ivan Sutherland used in 1963 to develop his groundbreaking graphic program, Sketchpad, was hardly faster than a skilled draftsman, but it foreshadowed impending revolution in drawing and erasing. Sutherland wrote in his dissertation: "It has turned out that the properties of a computer drawing are entirely different from a paper drawing not only because of the accuracy, ease of drawing, and speed of erasing...but also primarily because of the ability to move drawing parts around on a computer drawing without the need to erase them." The only way an architect could accomplish this at the time was to move the paper itself, lay another sheet of tracing paper down and draw anew.

Deciding which ideas to retain and which to eliminate is at the core of architectural judgment. Architects' studios are stuffed with sketches of designs that never found their way into built form but were valuable enough to save them from the electric eraser or the delete button. The eraser—along with all of its digital descendents—is the tool of redesign, as the pencil is a tool of design, allowing the architect to draw and redraw toward the solution. The drawing paper or the refreshed screen may appear to be blank, but the imagination of the architect, the ultimate external storage device, is filled with all of those ideas that have been moved to the "junkyard," "saved-as," "whited-out," exiled to Level 63, rolled up in a tube, but never entirely erased.

below, clockwise from top left
**Erasers, eraser shield,
electric eraser, and yellow
chuck**

opposite, left to right
**Correction fluid; selection of
leads, pencils, and pastels**

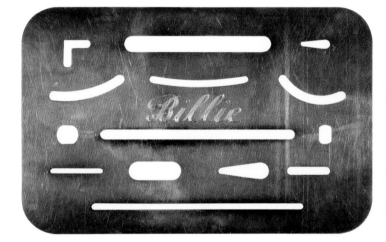

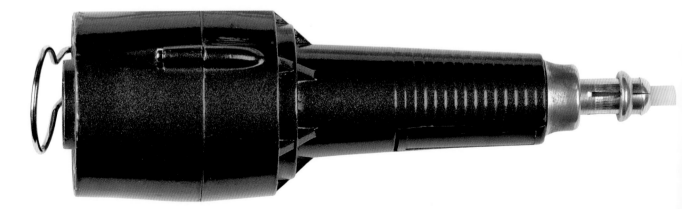

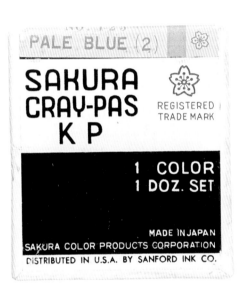

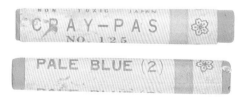

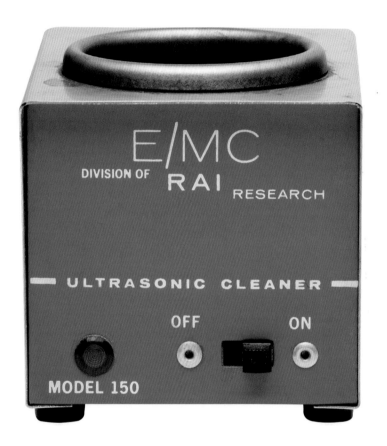

Many of the common tools present in the studio of Tod Williams Billie Tsien Architects (TWBTA) are on the verge of extinction. The unique sharpener, known as a lead pointer, once was commonplace on most drafting desks. The thin metal template is an eraser shield that protects everything but the mistake. The various tools for careful lettering of drawings are now rarely used—tools to make legible text on drawings, such as lettering guides and transfer sheets from which letters would be rubbed onto the paper, have been replaced by the computer. Some tools here are for cleaning other tools: the curiously named "pounce" and "bunny bag," or "scum bag," keep the drawing surface clean of smears and smudges. The ultrasonic cleaner was developed to address the primary nuisance of technical pens: clogged ink.

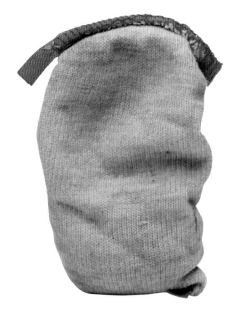

opposite, left
Ultrasonic cleaner

opposite, right
Lead pointer and lead holder

above
**Scum bag and Pounce
tracing cloth powder**

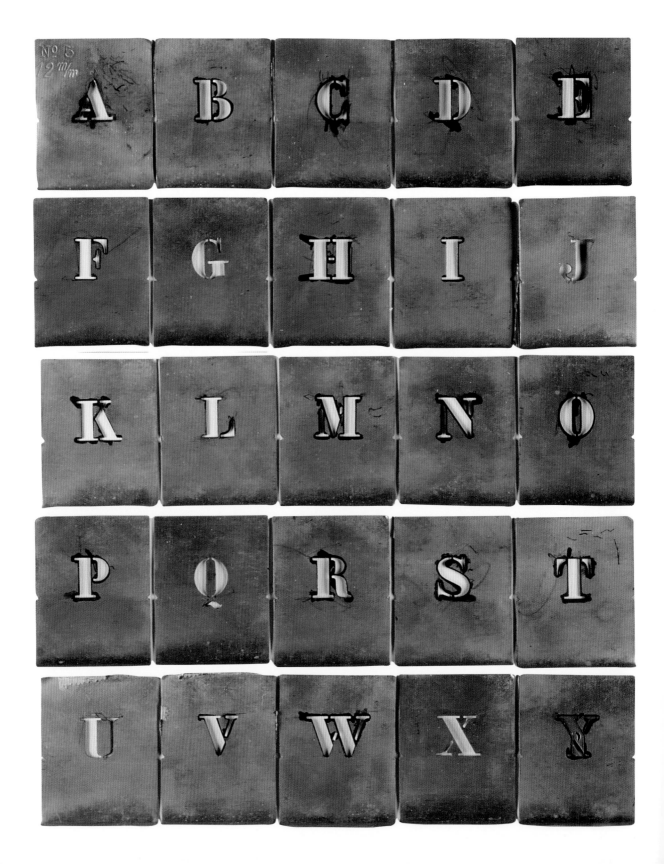

Collection of lettering
stencils

Technical pens with Kroy
lettering tool

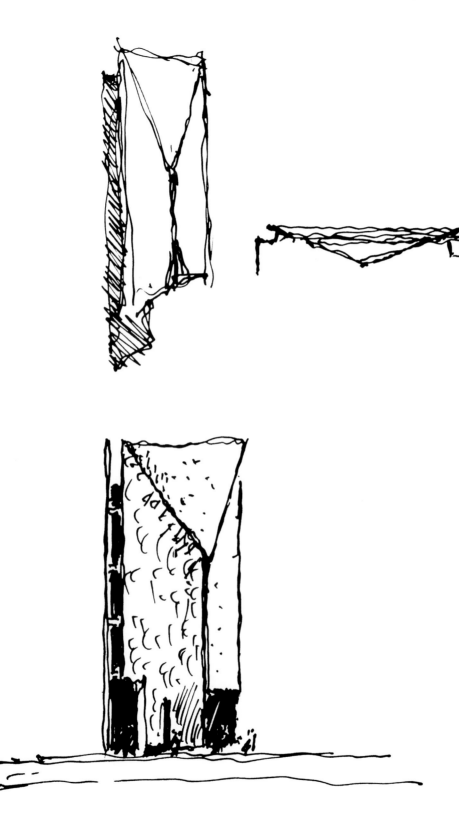

this page
**Initial design sketches,
Museum of American Folk
Art, New York, New York**
Tod Williams, 2001. Ink on
bond, 8½ x 11 in.

opposite
Assorted markers

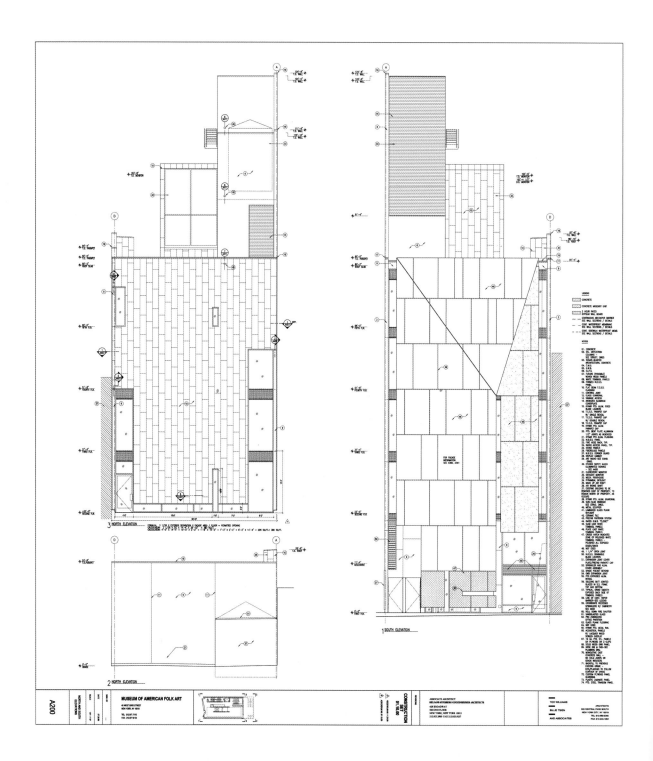

Software has an array of commands and buttons for various degrees of obliteration, each with an icon chosen to express most succinctly the action involved. SketchUp, the user-friendly three-dimensional drawing program by @Last Software, uses the familiar image of pencil with attached eraser as the icon for its erase button. SketchUp's eraser even behaves a bit like its image-sake: it can be used to rub out errors, soften edges, or smudge lines. AutoCAD uses this same icon for the simple erase command, but as a software suite for complex design and production projects, it has many more steps between making a line and deleting it. Lines and shapes can be erased, copied, moved, and offset; entire drawings can be filed, purged, and deleted. Even erasures can be unerased with the OOPS command. The help section does caution the user, however, that not even an extended OOPS can retrieve a purge. Autodesk's BIM software, Revit, takes a different approach to the graphics on the screen. A click on the demolish icon converts the cursor into a hammer, and any element touched by the hammer turns into dotted lines—virtual dust.

opposite
Construction document, Museum of American Folk Art
TWBTA, 2001. Printed on bond from digital file, 18 x 23 in. (half-sheet size).

above
Early sketch, Museum of American Folk Art
Billie Tsien, 2001. Pencil crayon on photo collage, 12 x 18 in.

Imagination and Building Beyond Tools

Phillip G. Bernstein, FAIA

Changing the ways that people express ideas has often led to profound changes in the ways we live. The invention of symbolic characters created writing, which made it possible to maintain records that early civilization needed to thrive. The invention of a practical printing press with moveable metal-alloy type created the modern book, resulted in widespread literacy, and unexpectedly replaced verbal storytelling with the written word as the method of passing learning between generations. An exponential increase in the spread of knowledge resulted. Today, the Internet makes that information widely accessible to most.

But history shows how difficult it can be to predict just how profoundly a new way of envisioning things can influence daily life, and today's technology accelerates this trend. Digital views of the world—be they instant assembly of information through Google or the blurring of reality in today's films and video games—change the way we see reality itself. The invention of new digital tools will bring fundamental changes to the ways architects create buildings—how architects realize the invention of their imaginations—and will undoubtedly have profound effects beyond the profession to the entire industry—effects we can only begin to imagine. Flat-panel computer screens are the new drafting table and the mouse and graphics tablet the new pencil and eraser (in some cases, the tablet computer—these technologies combine to allow the designer to draw directly on the screen). The large-scale printer produces the new blueprint, the laser cutter the new model. Technology has fulfilled its time-honored role by making an existing task faster and more efficient; computer-aided drafting (CAD) is now the norm.

Nonetheless, there is little conceptual difference between the analog tools that once sat on the architect's drafting table—pencils, triangles, compasses, scales—and their early digital counterparts in CAD. As with early word processors that mimicked the typewriter, the first generation of computerized design tools was intended to replicate hand drafting, replacing the hand-drawn line with its plotted counterpart. While for many practitioners the tools were effective time and money savers, the end product was the same: a two-dimensional drawing on paper. Those who chose to stay with their mechanical pencils and T-squares could effectively produce the same realization of their vision, albeit much more laboriously and with some diminished drawing accuracy. In fact, some assert that the crisp, clean computer-generated look of today's CAD tools obscures the same inaccuracies of their hand-drawn predecessors.

The implications of the switch to CAD are apparent only in the shapes and expressions of recent buildings. Architects' recent fascination with complex, curving, and swooping forms are as much a function of the ability to draw them with ease on a computer as any particular development in architectural style. That sweeping curved facade is much less intimidating to create when it will be generated by a circle command in CAD in lieu of a pencil, compass, and protractor.

Most of these analog instruments have been abandoned; hand drafting is considered antiquated. Their replacement by CAD is but the first step. A second-order shift in the way architects transform their imaginations into reality has been heralded by Building Information Modeling (BIM). Rather than use the power of technology simply to draw, a complex computer database combines form and function, appearance and operation, to create a complete digital model of a building. The core idea of BIM is to deliver information that is coordinated, internally consistent, and computable—that is, where the computer knows how to treat the aggregated data like a building that can behave in digital form as it will when constructed.

This tool completely redefines the concept of "representation." Architects, their consultants, and clients have a way to see not just how a building will look but how it will work, how it will consume energy, how it will affect the environment, and how proposed changes in building materials will affect structural integrity, the budget, and the schedule. Because of the effectiveness of interaction with a computer-simulated building, rather than with typical plan, section, and elevation drawings, BIM has reached acceptance among many architects today, and in some cases, the resultant collaborations have led to tremendous productivity gains.

In many ways, this change is more profound than that first transition from drafting tools to the original CAD. CAD-produced electronic drawings were logical successors to traditional hand drawings. With BIM, not only does the architect have a rich database of information to replace her pile of drawings (CAD-generated or otherwise) but that database can contain both the physical elements of the building—like doors, walls, and windows—and record their relationships. When choosing, for example, the dimensions of a given room, a BIM-based design can include not just the four enclosing walls, floor, and ceiling, but it locks those elements into a relationship that remains as the design is completed. This functionality is called "parametric design" and gives the designer a record of not just what she decided to create but why.

From another perspective, parametric design is even more provocative. Imagine our architect using the parametric characteristics of a wall or window—the rules that govern its dimensions and behavior—to carefully explore the best solution, one that looks good, maximizes lighting conditions, provides optimal views, saves the most energy, and

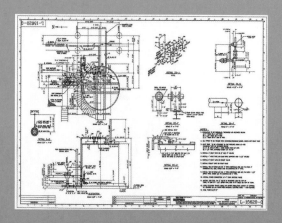

left
Early 2D CAD drawing

opposite
Views extracted from a Revit building information model, Freedom Tower, New York, New York
Skidmore, Owings & Merrill, projected completion 2010

meets budgetary requirements. Expand this concept to every element of the building as it comes into being digitally during design and the power of parametric BIM becomes apparent. The resulting data model of the building creates an unprecedented opportunity to provide a deep understanding of the design, one that can change the process by which we have created and constructed buildings—techniques that have not dramatically changed in thousands of years. By providing this kind of grasp of the totality of a design, BIM also establishes a context for changing the basic business processes that create a building, many of which are outdated, inefficient, and risky.

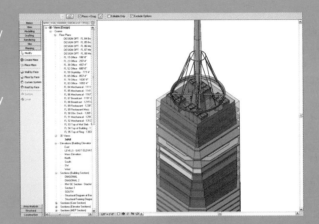

The potential to change the very culture of building, however, brings with it additional challenges. Technological opportunity precedes the underlying change in the culture of design and practice that it will catalyze. What often stands between the promise and the reality of the shift is hard-won tradition. Without the traditional barriers created by authorship and ownership of paper documents—even computer-generated ones—roles of various participants throughout the building process blur, responsibilities change, liability shifts, and new definitions of how the industry actually works are demanded.

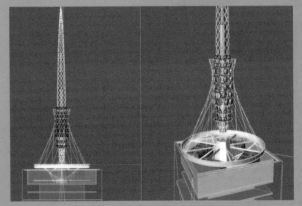

The typical method with which design information moves through the building process illuminates this issue. When an architect issues an official set of design documents for final building permit approval, she affixes her professional seal and signature to those drawings, which signifies that she supervised their creation, understands their content, and takes responsibility for their use. How is a digital project, however, "signed and sealed?" What does it mean to take responsibility for design information that has been aggregated in BIM and comes from multiple sources, like engineers and product manufacturers? Is "a drawing" even a meaningful idea in this context? Who is the actual "author" of that information?

More significant is the question of what is called "professional standard of care," the basic legal criterion to which architects (and all professionals) are held in their work.

**Rendering created from
daylighting analysis and
numerically quantifiable
pseudocolor intensity
radiosity model**
Produced from a Revit building
information model

This standard is generally defined as "what a competent architect in similar circumstances would have done." Only by comparison with competent action can an architect be found to have been negligent. The measure of care is, by definition, backward looking: the only way to reliably determine competence is to look at what other architects have done in the past. Implementing BIM with all its implications for collaboration, new information, and new ways of working requires the architect to depart from the comfort zone of tradition and try things that cannot be measured by the standard of care.

These are but two examples of how the business infrastructure of the building industry that has evolved from long traditions must change. They imply that basic definitions of roles, responsibilities, and deliverable work products need to evolve, along with the legal instruments like contracts and insurance policies that support them. Until these underlying business issues are resolved, BIM's full benefit to the building process today cannot be realized. For architects, the central question remains: given the enormous benefits, are they willing to break from tradition to change?

Change in architectural implements is inevitable because of the demands society makes on its buildings and the economic demands within the building industry itself. BIM offers the building industry its first chance to dramatically modernize in more than a century. One of the most significant changes is the elimination of the paper drawing as the medium of information exchange between participants in the design and build processes. Despite the long use of computers in the initial design of a structure, even the most innovative designs have been reduced to paper form when it comes time to send them to the structural engineer or the building constructor and various contractors. Paper's limitations are significant, and well known. For example, as mapmakers discovered as far back as Ptolemy, representing a three-dimensional object on a two-dimensional surface requires compromises that skew the image or, at best, demands extensive inferential reasoning. Additionally, the sheer size and complexity of even the simplest building requires extensive abstraction, short hand, and a special language of plan, section, elevation, and detail in its representation. In a simpler time, Brunelleschi designed the dome over the cathedral in Florence without drawings, only using a large wooden model. In some ways, BIM returns us to that vivid approach.

Errors are easily introduced by humans during copying and continue to replicate themselves through successive generations of a document. In traditional design, the same building element is often represented many times in a set of drawings. The front door of a house appears in the first floor plan, the front elevation view, a detailed plan of the entrance hall, a view of the interior wall of the hall, details of the trim and hardware, and the listing (schedule) of all the doors in the project. Failing to make sure that door is consistently shown throughout the drawings is a common problem. Adjustments are typically made by designating changes to the drawing. This is an inherently error-prone process, with consequences that can range from the minor to the catastrophic.

Because a digital model contains all the information necessary to produce any representation of a building needed—from a traditional elevation to an energy-usage analysis—it is the database that forms the foundation of information exchange among the parties. It renders paper obsolete and can eliminate many of these costly errors. A single copy of this database can be maintained and shared with everyone involved in the creation of a building and changes are instantly accessible. That door described above is "designed" once, inserted into the BIM database, and displays itself accurately in every relevant view, digital or otherwise. A single model recognizes if the change is feasible and how it affects everything from the potential interference of two building members to what materials need to be ordered for the job site. When paper is needed, it is generated not by hand, but as a report from a consistent database.

We are rapidly approaching the point where the drawing, the paper image, is about to be viewed as quaint as some of the tools of yesteryear. In the not-too-distant future, we will have high-resolution computer screens or dynamic digital "paper" that will be as flexible and portable as analog paper for viewing representations. The day is not far off when even the contractor in the pickup truck with his dog in the back will have a lightweight, large-scale high-resolution digital "paper screen" rolled under his arm.

Design and construction are not linear activities; rather, they are rife with random injections of information, outliers, and serendipity. The change to BIM is more than the elimination of paper; it is a radical change in the interconnection between design and construction, the studio and the shop floor, and the model and the construction site. Architects and designers tend to work today as they have for centuries, in a relentlessly iterative fashion that proceeds sequentially from design to fabrication to installation, where changes traverse the line back to their origins and begin their inevitable trip back along the same path.

BIM aims to conceive a truly integrated practice that combines architecture, engineering, and construction to see the creation of a building as a single, collaborative process, one that considers the building not as a discrete entity fixed in time but as a living thing within its dynamic surroundings. Industry professionals have been known to declare that buildings are the only modern products that are constructed as full-scale prototypes at full cost. Model-based design gives designers the opportunity to understand how a building will actually behave before it is built and brings the profession into the twenty-first century.

The current model of the building process is filled with tension and conflict, with architects and engineers typically providing services (the design) and contractors providing products (the constructed result). In an integrated approach, these roles will blur, necessitating new definitions of responsibility: What are the limits of accountability for each participant in the building process, especially the architect, the engineer, and the contractor, when those functions are integrated through a common digital vision of the design?

When one builds from a collaborative digital model, it is unclear who assumes responsibility for failure and for success. BIM technology may be able to identify the specific author of a piece of design data, but it cannot track the decision-making process that brought it into existence. As shared information and joint decisions soften the lines of responsibility, the very definition of competent practice will change in the face of the new construct.

Business abhors uncertainty, creating a natural barrier to the adoption of BIM despite the marketplace pressures to make the change. Yet in an industry with a tendency for low profit margins and great vulnerability to economic swings, the opportunities of the new paradigm are

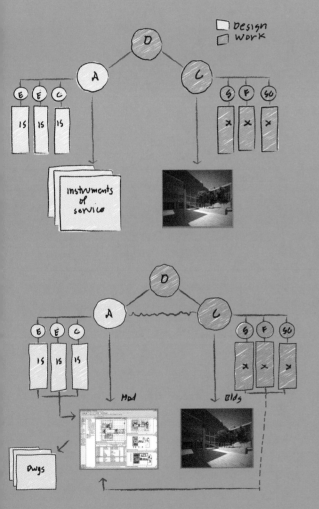

enormous. The value of the data created by BIM alone in creating better and less-wasteful buildings, more predictable outcomes, more precise cost estimates, even more sustainable design, must translate into higher value services and greater financial compensation to all the players in the process. Perhaps the era of low margins (and lower salaries) might come to an end.

It is no small matter to change roles, responsibilities, obligations, and processes that have been in place since the Renaissance. But in an industry ripe for reform, the change is worth the risk. The newest technologies offer a profound transition from the ancient traditions of drawing-to-building; our imagination must be applied not just to the design of buildings but also to the processes that create architecture itself.

top
Current Process: Architects deliver design; contractors deliver work
Phillip G. Bernstein, undated

bottom
Integrated process: traditional roles blur
Phillip G. Bernstein, undated

Conclusion

Improvisations, Instruments, and Algorithms

William J. Mitchell

Drawing with a free hand is like dancing on paper. It can be as energetic as krumping or a more sedate and reflective activity, like, in the words of Paul Klee, taking a line for a walk. The result is a trace of improvised motion. Lines have attack and decay. At each point, they register the momentary direction, speed, pressure, and angle of a marker engaging a surface; their numerous, subtle variations carrying meaning.

Making a freehand drawing is a performance, and it helps to have a skilled performer's repertoire of practiced moves. The performance may be private and silent, like solitary prayer. It may be part of a dialogue, as when a critic picks up a pencil to explain an idea to a student. It may even be public and highly theatrical, as when a professor declaims to a packed auditorium while sketching on a blackboard. But whatever the circumstances, it is impossible to repeat identically. For those who were present at the unique enactment, the complex marks that remain trigger memories of a context, a subject, and perhaps a conversation.

Producing a drawing with instruments is an altogether more disciplined, modularized, replicable activity. The task is always broken down into discrete, standardized steps executed with mechanical devices, often tracing lines with straightedges and arcs with compasses but also producing ellipses, parabolas, and other more complex shapes. The resulting marks are not to be read as records of an artist's hand in motion, but as symbols standing for timeless Platonic abstractions. Accidents and imperfections of execution, then, are just meaningless blemishes.

Euclid's beautiful constructions are specified sequences of these elementary operations. To erect a perpendicular bisector on a given straight line, for example, you must:

(1) strike an arc from one end of the line; (2) keeping the radius constant, strike an arc from the other end; (3) construct a straight line through the two intersection points of the arcs. Euclid's constructions permit the formation of perpendiculars, parallels, and other well-defined relationships of lines and arcs and more complex figures, such as equilateral triangles, squares, rectangles, and trapezoids. Using the same means, these figures can be assembled into still larger compositions recursively. In other words, elementary drafting instruments, together with Euclid's constructions, rigorously define a graphic vocabulary and syntax. With the necessary sequence of discrete standard operations, any competent draftsperson can execute the sequence to produce exactly the same result. The sequence is, then, an algorithm.

In drafting instruments, useful abstractions may be embodied in the mechanics of specialized devices. T-squares and parallel rules, for example, allow the quick construction of parallels, and wooden or plastic triangles enable the addition of perpendiculars. Drafting instruments not only imply the graphic vocabulary and syntax but also some of the abstractions that structure practical graphic construction processes.

When computer graphics technology emerged in the 1960s, the most fundamental idea underlying it was that a straight line, an arc, or any other sort of curve could be described as the trace of a point moving across a surface or through space. The shape of the curve could be described parametrically by means of formulas that expressed coordinates as functions of time. Procedures containing these formulas became the computer-graphics equivalents of straightedges, compasses, and French curves. Higher-level procedures, which were built from these, implemented

Euclid's constructions. The instructions for production of complete drawings could be encoded as sequences of calls, with appropriate parameters, to the available procedures. These sequences could be executed repeatedly, even carried out on different computers, to produce exactly the same results. A computer, instead of a draftsperson, executed the algorithm.

The idiosyncrasies of the artist's hand were now completely eliminated from the process. Drawings could be specified by typing in commands and numbers, or by pointing and clicking with a mouse and a cursor. A speech interface allowed verbal commands to talk a drawing into existence. The method with which commands were given was no longer important so long as the necessary symbols got into the data structure—a reduction of the drawing to its Platonic essence.

Computer graphics and computer-aided design systems have enormously extended their ranges of graphic primitives and higher-level procedures. Relying upon software skills rather than mechanical ingenuity, graphics programmers first replicated the functions of traditional drafting instruments and then went far beyond them. This has made a wider graphic vocabulary available to designers, together with a more elaborate syntax—in all, a richer and potentially more expressive graphic and spatial language. The effects, as any observer of current architectural production can see, have been profound.

Something has, of course, been lost. Fine drawing instruments are wonderfully crafted, beautiful objects. They feel good in the hand, and there is a particular satisfaction—which older architects can still recall—in their swift and skilled use. But, for those with eyes to see, there is

something to take their place. The code of an elegantly constructed graphics algorithm has an austere, functional beauty that can take your breath away. Perhaps, one day, the National Building Museum will nostalgically exhibit the software tools of yesteryear.

Bibliography

Ackerman, James S. *Origins, Imitations, Conventions: Representation in the Visual Arts.* Cambridge, MA: MIT Press, 2002.

Adams, George. *Geometrical and Graphical Essays.* London: W. Glendenning, 1803.

Benjamin, Walter. "The Work of Art in the Age of Mechanical Reproduction." In *Walter Benjamin: Illuminations: Essays and Reflections,* edited by Hannah Arendt. New York: Schocken Books, 1986.

Evans, Robin. *Translations from Drawings to Building and Other Essays.* Cambridge, MA: MIT Press, 1997.

Hambly, Maya. *Drawing Instruments: 1580–1980.* New York: Sotheby's Publications, 1988.

Kubler, George. *The Shape of Time: Remarks on the History of Things.* New Haven and London: Yale University Press, 1962.

Lambert, Susan. *Reading Drawings: An Introduction to Looking at Drawings.* London: Susan Lambert and the Victoria & Albert Museum, 1984.

Lindsey, Bruce. *Digital Gehry: Material Resistance, Digital Construction.* Boston: Birkhäuser, 2001.

Mitchell, William. *The Logic of Architecture: Design, Computation, and Cognition.* Cambridge, MA: MIT Press, 1990.

Nicholson, Peter. *The New Practical Builder and Workman's Companion: Containing a Full Display.* London: Thomas Kelly, 1823.

Peterson, Ivars. "From Graphic to Plastic." *Science News* 140, no. 6 (1991): 72–73.

Salmon, William. *Palladio Londonensis.* London: S. Birt, 1745.

Stanley, William Ford. *A Descriptive Treatise on Mathematical Drawing Instruments.* London: E. and F. N. Spon, 1866, 1888, 1900.

Sutherland, Ivan. "Sketchpad: The First Interactive Computer Graphics." Ph.D. diss., MIT, 1963.

Additional Sources

Design Tools: a Collector's Perspective and an Architect's Odyssey

Albrecht, Andreas. *Instrument zur Architectur.* Nuermberg: Ludwig Lochner, 1622.

Bion, N. (Nicholas). *Construction and Principal Uses of Mathematical Instruments: Including Thirty Folio Illustrations of Several Instruments.* Translated by Edmund Stone. Mendham, NJ: The Astragal Press, 1995. First published 1723 by H. W. for J. Senex and W. Taylor.

Hambly, Maya. *Drawing Instruments: Their History, Purpose and Use for Architectural Drawing.* London: The Architectural Association, 1982.

Heather, J. F. *Mathematical Instruments.* London: Crosby Lockwood & Co., 1877.

Holbrook, Mary. *Science Preserved.* London: The Science Museum, 1992.

Kirby, Joshua. *The Description & Use of a New Instrument Called the Architectonic Sector.* London: R. Francklin, 1761.

Martin, Benjamin. *Description and Use of a Case of Mathematical Instruments.* London, 1771.

Robertson, John. *Treatise of Such Math. Instr. as are Usually Put into a Portable Case.* London, 1747.

Schillinger, Klaus. *Zeicheninstrumente.* Dresden, 1990.

Scott, Michael. *Drawing Instruments 1850–1950.* Aylesbury, England: Shire Publications, 1986.

The Lead Pencil: Lever of the Architect's Imagination

Ayres, James. *The Artist's Craft: A History of Tools, Techniques and Materials.* Oxford: Phaidon, 1985.

Bachelard, Gaston. *Right to Dream.* Translated by J. A. Underwood. Dallas: Dallas Institute Publications, Dallas Institute of Humanities and Culture, 1988.

Bambach, Carmen. *Drawing and Painting in the Italian Renaissance Workshop: Theory and Practice, 1300–1600.* Cambridge: Cambridge University Press, 1999.

Berkeley, George. *Essay Towards a New Theory of Vision.* Dublin, 1709.

Booker, Peter. *A History of Engineering Drawing.* London: Northgate, 1979. First published 1963 by Chatto & Windus.

Cigliano, Jan, and George Hartman, eds. *The Pencil Points Reader: A Journal for the Drafting Room, 1920–1943.* New York: Princeton Architectural Press, 2004.

Deleuze, Gilles, and Felix Guattari. "Balance Sheet: Program for Desiring Machines." *Semiotext(e)* 2, no. 3 (1977): 117–35.

Ferguson, Eugene. *Engineering and the Mind's Eye.* Cambridge, MA: MIT Press, 1992.

Frascari, Marco. "The Drafting Knife and Pen." In *Implementing Architecture: Exposing the Paradigm Surrounding the Implements and Implementation of Architecture,* edited by Rob Miller. Atlanta: Nexus Press, 1988.

———. "Architectural Ideas…Put Them on Paper!" Lecture, Devices of Design Symposium sponsored by Canadian Centre for Architecture and the Daniel Langlois Foundation for Art, Science, and Technology, Montreal, Canada, November 18, 2004.

French, Thomas. *A Manual of Engineering Drawing.* 2nd ed., 1918.

Henderson, Kathryn. *On Line and On Paper: Visual Representation, Visual Culture, and Computer Graphics in Design Engineering.* Cambridge, MA: MIT Press, 1999.

Higbee, F. G. "The Development of Graphical Representation." *Journal of Engineering Drawing* 22 (April 1958): 14–22.

Kahn, Louis. *Louis Kahn: Writings, Lectures, Interviews.* Edited by Alessandra Latour. New York: Rizzoli, 1991.

Le Corbusier. *Precisions: On the Present State of Architecture and City Planning.* Translated by Edith Schreiber Aujame. Cambridge, MA: MIT Press, 1991.

Lomazzo, Giovanni. *Trattato dell'arte de la pittura.* Oxford: J. Barnes, 1598. Translated by Richard Haydocke as *A Tracte Containing the Artes of Curious Paintinge, Carving and Buildinge.*

Loos, Adolf. "Architecture (1910)." In *On Architecture.* Selected and Introduced by Adolf and Daniel Opel. Translated by Michael Mitchell. Riverside, CA: Ariadne Press, 2002.

Menocal, Narciso G., and Robert C. Twombly. *Louis Sullivan: The Poetry of Architecture.* New York: W. W. Norton, 2000.

Peacham, Henry. *The Art of Drawing with the Pen and Limming in Water Colours.* London: R. Braddock, 1607.

Piner, Richard, et. al. "Dip-Pen Nanolithography." *Science* 283 (January 29, 1999): 661–63.

Petroski, Henry. *The Pencil: A History of Design and Circumstance.* New York: Knopf, 1997.

Pratt, Sir Roger. *The Architecture of Sir Roger Pratt, Charles II's Commissioner for the Rebuilding of London after the Great Fire.* Edited by R. T. (Robert Theodore) Gunther, Oxford: J. John at the University Press, 1928.

Price, C. M. "A Study in Scholastic Architecture." *Architectural Record* 35 (January 1914): 20.

Robertson, John. *A Treatise of Mathematical Drawing Instruments.* 3rd edition. London, 1775.

Ruskin, John. *The Elements of Drawing.* New York: J. Wiley & Sons, 1881.

———. *The Ethics of Dust: Ten Lectures to Little Housewives on the Elements of Crystallization.* London: Frank F. Lovell and Company, 1866.

Sullivan, Louis H. *A System of Architectural Ornament According with a Philosophy of Man's Powers.* New York: Press of the American Institute of Architects, Inc., 1922.

Thoreau, Henry David. *Journal.* John C. Broderick, general editor. Edited by Elizabeth Hall Witherell, et al. Princeton: Princeton University Press, 1981.

Tunick, Susan. *Terra-Cotta Skyline: New York's Architectural Ornament.* New York: Princeton Architectural Press, 1997.

Watrous, James. *The Craft of Old Master Drawings.* Madison: University of Wisconsin Press, 1957.

Whalley, Joyce. *Writing Implements and Accessories: From the Roman Stylus to the Typewriter.* Detroit: Gale Research Co., 1975.

Exhibition Acknowledgments

Curator: Susan C. Piedmont-Palladino

Curatorial Associate: Reed Haslach

Exhibition design: Knowtis Design, Alexandria, Virginia

Exhibition advisory committee:

Carol Bartz, Chairman of the Board, President and Chief Executive Officer, Autodesk, Inc., San Rafael, California

Greg Bentley, Chief Executive Officer, Bentley Systems, Inc., Exton, Pennsylvania

Phillip G. Bernstein, FAIA, Vice President, Building Solutions Division, Autodesk, Inc., Waltham, Massachusetts

Dr. Paul Emmons, Associate Professor of Architecture, Virginia Polytechnic Institute and State University, Alexandria, Virginia

Dr. Marco Frascari, GT Ward Professor of Architecture, Virginia Polytechnic Institute and State University, Alexandria, Virginia

Robert W. Holleyman, II, President and CEO, Business Software Alliance, Washington, D.C.

Peggy Kidwell, Curator of Mathematics, Division of Technology and Society, National Museum of American History, Washington, D.C.

William Mitchell, Dean, School of Architecture and Planning, Massachusetts Institute of Technology, Cambridge, Massachusetts

C. Ford Peatross, Curator, Architecture, Design & Engineering Collections, Library of Congress, Washington, D.C.

E. Phillip Read, Senior Project Consultant, Autodesk Consulting, Waltham, Massachusetts

Anne Ritchie, Gallery Archivist, National Gallery of Art, Washington, D.C.

Huw Roberts, AIA, CSI, Global Marketing Director, Bentley Building, Bentley Systems, Inc., Exton, Pennsylvania

David Thompson, AIA, Vice President, RTKL Associates, Washington, D.C.

Bradley E. Workman, AIA, Vice President, Bentley Building, Bentley Systems, Inc., Exton, Pennsylvania

Norbert W. Young, Jr., FAIA, President, McGraw-Hill Construction, New York, New York

The exhibition TOOLS OF THE IMAGINATION was made possible by the generous support of Autodesk, Inc.; Bentley Systems, Inc.; McGraw-Hill Construction; Business Software Alliance; Microsoft, Inc.; Hewlett-Packard Company; Fross Zelnick Lehrman & Zissu, P.C.; and Norbert W. Young, Jr.

Image Credits

Contributor Biographies

Susan C. Piedmont-Palladino is a curator at the National Building Museum, most recently of the TOOLS OF THE IMAGINATION exhibition. She is an architect and an associate professor of Architecture at Virginia Polytechnic Institute and State University's Washington-Alexandria Architecture Center, where she earned an MArch degree. Her first book, *Devil's Workshop: 25 Years of Jersey Devil Architecture*, was published by Princeton Architectural Press in 1997.

Reed Haslach is a curatorial associate at the National Building Museum. She holds an MA from George Washington University. She has coordinated several past National Building Museum exhibitions including Masonry Variations, TOOLS OF THE IMAGINATION, and The Green House: New Directions in Sustainable Architecture and Design.

Phillip G. Bernstein is an architect and Vice President of the Building Solutions Division, Autodesk, Inc. He holds an MArch from Yale University and was formerly with the office of Cesar Pelli & Associates. Bernstein teaches at the Yale School of Architecture, writes and lectures on project management and technology, and works nationally on practice and education issues.

Howard S. Decker, FAIA, is the former Chief Curator of the National Building Museum and practices architecture with Ehrenkrantz Eckstut & Kuhn. He holds an MArch from the University of Illinois at Chicago and was a founding principal of DLK Architecture in Chicago.

Paul Emmons is an architect who publishes and lectures internationally on his research in architectural representation. Currently an associate professor at the Washington-Alexandria Architecture Center of Virginia Polytechnic Institute and State University, Emmons holds a PhD from the University of Pennsylvania. He dedicates his essay to his father, who first introduced him to the wonder of drawing with the pencil.

William J. Mitchell is a Professor of Architecture and Media Arts and Sciences at the Massachusetts Institute of Technology. He was formerly dean of the School of Architecture and Planning and head of the Program in Media Arts and Sciences, both at MIT. He holds an MED from Yale University and an MA from the University of Cambridge.

David V. Thompson is an architect and Vice President / Public Sector Leader at RTKL Associates, Inc., a global design practice. He holds an MArch from Texas A&M University. He has been a member of the Scientific Instrument Society and a collector of drawing instruments and related books since 1998.